A Love Letter
to the Lost

Bekah DeiFilia

ISBN 979-8-88751-687-5 (paperback)
ISBN 979-8-88751-688-2 (digital)

Christian Faith Publishing
832 Park Avenue
Meadville, PA 16335
www.christianfaithpublishing.com

Printed in the United States of America

I T'S DARK.

    I'm conscious, but I'm afraid to open my eyes. Am I breathing? I think so.

I focus on my breath.

It's shallow, but I'm fairly certain, present.

I focus on my pulse.

I can feel it, but only in my chest. I try to push it out to my limbs from there. Am I still in my body? I clench my hands, my feet. It feels like my body.

Where am I? I'm afraid to move. If I move, I'll start to understand where I am. My brain is foggy. I try to remember what happened. My mouth has a remnant taste of blood. There is a pain that starts to rise near my stomach, and I can feel sweat start to form all over me as my pulse grows more palpable.

Am I in heaven? I can't be. There's not supposed to be any pain there. Is it purgatory? Or worse?

My memory starts to come back.

I was sitting alone in my bedroom. It was silent, like it is in this moment. I had them strewn across my bedspread. I had spent hours staring at each one. I had counted them over and over. There were ninety-eight.

I wanted there to be anything—a phone call, a knock on my door. I would've settled for the cat pawing at my door as a reason that would've been enough to hold me back. But there was nothing.

I count them again.

Ninety-eight. The number is as consistent as the gnawing emptiness that captivates my every waking moment of existence.

Ninety-eight. I've romanticized this moment for months, longing for it like a long-awaited homecoming. The medications made no difference. The drugs would work in the moment, but when they wore off, I always just ended up feeling worse. The self-harm had the same effect. Every therapist I saw just magnified all the feelings I couldn't seem to work out.

Ninety-eight. Far less than the number of days I had spent trying to fight this. Far more than the number of people who would be at my funeral, if there even was one. Ninety-eight. Everything I did was never enough. It was never right. The only thing I could ever get "right" was repeatedly ruining whatever situation I was in and letting people down. I am a failure. No one could ever love me. I am worthless. I'm doing my family a favor by finally acting on this. I was an accident anyways, and I need to lighten their burden.

There are ninety-eight.

I take the first one…am I really doing this?

I take two more. I want to start crying, but I feel like there's nothing inside of me to come out. I want to scream for help, but my throat is coarse, and when I open my mouth, there's just silence that meets me. I gather a small handful and swallow them.

Eighty-two. I'm breathing as if I'm standing on the edge of a cliff, staring at the rocks below. I gather another handful and repeat.

Sixty-eight. What will the morning be like? Who will be the first person to walk in to find me? How quickly will everyone feel relief now that they don't have to try to deal with me anymore?

Forty-four. Will it hurt? Will my heart just stop in my sleep? Will God even consider letting me into heaven? No one loves me. I shouldn't expect Him to. I am a monster.

Twenty-six. I have no value.

Twelve. I'm a screwup even for waiting this long to do this.

Zero.

I still haven't opened my eyes. The pain in my abdomen is growing stronger. Maybe I'm at heaven's gates and I'm feeling pain because I haven't entered yet. The pain is in places of my body I have never consciously felt before. It's growing stronger by the millisecond. I don't want to open my eyes. I don't want to exist anywhere. I just want it to stop.

No matter where I am, I'm going to have to open my eyes. I'm going to have to see what happened. I have to see if I finally followed through with anything successfully. Like plunging into ice water, I force myself conscious into whatever world I ended up in.

It's blurry at first as I look around. Is this real? It can't be real. No, no, this can't be real! I cry out to a god I hope exists as the reality of where I am sinks in. My body produces a moan that harmonizes with the cries of the damned as the deepest sorrow I have ever felt consumes me and renders me motionless.

The pain is unbearable. I feel as if my teeth are going to shatter from the pressure of me involuntarily gnashing them.

It's still dark in my bedroom. I debate getting my razor to rightfully finish what I started. I know it's still far too messy, and I doubt the smell of blood would ever truly leave the grain of the wood floor in this room.

My thought process is viciously halted by the overwhelming need to retch. I manage to get myself to the toilet and spend the next hour vomiting violently and sobbing. It feels as if someone has attached a knife to the end of a power drill and has managed to place it at the center of my kidneys to work to destroy them from the inside out. It is the worst physical pain I have ever experienced.

I emerge from the bathroom to find my mom waiting for me on the couch, like she always would when we were little kids, waiting to ask if I was okay.

I want to tell her everything. I should probably get to a hospital. But just like so many times before, as I open my mouth to try to form the words, all that meets me is silence. All I can do is cry.

She hugs me as I struggle through the words, "I must have the flu." I tell her I'm in a lot of pain and I just need to lie down. Reluctantly, she agrees, and I go back into my failed coffin of a bedroom.

My mind is still foggy as I try to grasp what is real. I am still alive.

I live in the middle of nowhere, Wisconsin.

I have achieved the highest level of incompetence by failing to kill myself.

Thanksgiving is in four days.

I am the most lost I have ever been.

I am in desperate need of anything to be a savior.

From this point forward, as far as I can
tell, I have basically two options.
One—try to accept this "savior" that my entire upbringing
to date has tried to cram down my throat. And really,
if we're being honest, look where that just got me.
Two—screw it. Apparently, I can't die.
How far can I push this theory?

CONTENTS

HOW DID I
END UP HERE?

A S I SIT HERE BEGINNING this journey with you, it's notable that this current moment in time is almost a to-the-day anniversary of the moment in my life you just relived with me.

That was me fifteen years ago.

And to be honest, at that moment in time, I never imagined I would be a thirty-year-old version of myself, period. In any way, shape, or form—other than in an urn.

At that moment in time, the idea of feeling genuinely and deeply loved was such a fragile and foreign concept to me. It felt more like I was living my life as an extra on everyone else's main stage. In fact, I felt like the outsider in pretty much every aspect of my entire life—my community, my church, my school, my family, and with my friends. I felt like the last thought on the entire world's mind.

At that moment in time, all I had learned to take to heart was the weight of everything that held me down. The only things I had learned to hold tight to were the things that were used as weapons against me. I had learned to get wounded and stay wounded, and I had learned to revel in that way of living. Like a pack of wolves going in for the kill, so was my intensity for reimagining and reliving each deep-seated memory I'd allow to haunt me.

At that moment in time, I really don't think I *truly* believed that there was anything that could get me out of where I was.

I wasn't just lost. I was hurting, desolate, hopeless, and flatlining. And yet I mostly continued to choose to live that way for the next ten years.

Why?

It's easy to ask that question in this context. I've no doubt you know enough to know that life isn't always black-and-white, no matter how much we wish it to be otherwise. If it were as simple as identifying bad when you see it then just avoiding it, shouldn't that be enough of an easy formula to avoid most pain throughout life? But so many of us are unaware of our faulty and cracked lens we just never had a chance. We're used to it by now.

And we've gotten carried away in our naming rights. We replant the same bad habits in different places, expecting them to grow into different results since we've given it a different name. Sadly, lemon seeds still only produce lemon trees. Yet we feel unjustly haunted by things we thought we'd buried.

So what's the difference between this moment in time now versus the moment in time where you met me at the beginning of this journey? Honestly, it can really all be boiled down to one simple answer.

Hold on a minute though, you don't even know me. And odds are really pretty good that I don't even know you. So what's in my life now that I was desperately searching for through some of the darkest moments of my existence? And why would you, a likely stranger, be encompassed with such slowly eroding curiosity that you would grace the pages of my presence for the remainder of this voyage together?

As I've gotten older, I've grown to value depth in the relationships I have in my life. You can have the most outstanding creation built in the history of mankind, but if it's built on sand, it's going to crumble. Depth is important in real quality.

I want to share with you the single biggest thing that has radically transformed the definition of who I am, how I view myself, and how I live my life. But I know it wouldn't mean as much coming from a stranger.

So to remedy that, I'm going to share some things with you. As I sit here typing that sentence out for the first time and realizing the gravity it holds, I can already feel my heart start to race in my chest. You see, I've got these battle wounds. A very real burden of shame and regret that I've seemingly no other option than to carry with me all the moments of my life.

Maybe that kind of feeling is somewhat familiar to you? Or maybe a feeling of being haunted by something you had to go through hits closer to home? Something that made you feel blindsided and left you damaged before you could even comprehend what just happened? Have you ever been there?

I'm going to share some things with you that, up until this moment, very few other people have ever heard. I'm guessing a lot of people I know would be pretty surprised to hear that this is the life I've lived. I very rarely share it because it's a story I've been too ashamed to put words to.

But I believe there is undeniable power in vulnerability. And I'm not so arrogant to believe that I'm the only one on the planet who has ever scraped through those trenches I indwelled. And I refuse to believe the lie any longer that tries to tell me those places are too dark to ever shine a light on again or too shameful to ever speak out and attach my name to.

No matter what it looks like for you personally, we all have things in our past that constantly fight to be the loudest voice in what defines us.

For years and years, I desperately searched to find a voice that, even if it be a fleeting wisp on a back wind, felt or sounded anything like love. I wanted to understand what that felt like when it genuinely flowed through you. Would happiness follow after? Oh, how I wanted to know! How I was desperate to find that, to feel that.

But every time my search failed, I'd end up going back to what was familiar, because at least there was familiarity in the trenches. And the more times I'd go back, the more elaborate the tunnel design within them became. It was like, as I'd try digging my way out, when I'd catch a glimpse of some light, the light would become consumed by darkness, disorienting me and sending me further in the wrong direction.

I'd try to use the things I found in the depths to help me get out. I'll go more into detail about those things in the pages to come. But in case you're there now, in your own trenches, let me just share with you a takeaway that will always be true for all of us: just because you find something that helps you in the moment does not mean it is good for you, and it does not mean it's something you should hold on to.

Sometimes we end up in a trench through entirely no fault of our own. It's the actions of other people in our lives—people we may even love and trust—that land us in places we find ourselves desperate to get out of. Other times, we find ourselves clawing at the same slick, muddied walls of our own personal prison with no one else to blame but ourselves.

Whether it's a distant spouse or child, a shattered career, the demise of a long-hoped-for dream, or the endless resounding pangs of loneliness deep within you, we all have something that leeches onto the core of who we are. Maybe it's heavier than that for you. Maybe your distance was created by death. Maybe injustice has gutted you and taken years away from you that were supposed to be filled with joy, and now there's nothing but ash and rubble. And now it's all you can do just to agonizingly pull yourself out of bed in the morning. Hope? It's a laughable concept at this point.

The name of our trenches may vary, but the feelings we share when we're down there don't. The trenches are isolating. Their purpose is to make you feel like you'll never leave, like you don't *deserve* to leave. They can become a well-oiled cycle of fall, get back up, try again, fall, get back up, try again, fall, sit back up, eventually try again. Fall, make camp for the night. Get back up, fall, improve your tent.

Eventually, it just feels easier to decorate your tent than to face what's still defeated you time after time. We start to learn trench mentality and all the intricacies of that broken way of thinking and living. Our eyes start to adapt to the darkness, and we start to see and pick up things that were meant to stay buried.

"But this is home now," we convince ourselves. "And this is my toolbox. If I can't get out, shouldn't I learn to use what I have down here?"

That kind of broken logic kept me well below sea level for almost half my life. It created a Stockholm syndrome in me that I not only watered but protected above all else.

So how are we supposed to identify the things that will only hurt us more versus the things that will actually help us get up and get out of the trenches for good? How do we begin to turn around weeks, months, or years of broken cycles? Where do you even start when it feels like you've tried everything within your power already? Or how do you even begin to believe it's worth trying even one more time?

I'm compelled to share this all with you because for years, I believed with everything in me that I would never leave my trenches. But I learned a secret a little while ago that totally blew my mind.

I had believed a lie.

"What, that's it? You believed a lie? And now all your problems are solved?" I can imagine the questions going through some of your minds right now.

No, no one waved a magic wand and solved all the problems in my life. But realizing I was putting my trust in a lie was the beginning of my way out.

And even if you've already got a mansion set up down there, even if you've named it and made it your own, at the end of the day, you were never meant to stay there.

It does not matter what you have done, what has been done to you, or what kind of open wounds you're still trying to protect, your story was not ever meant to end at the bottom of that trench.

If no one has told you this before, let me be the first. No matter who you are, no matter what you've done, no matter what you're still going through, you do not deserve to stay in that trench! There is a way out, and it's been waiting for you this whole time.

There is hope. You might not feel it just yet, but I promise you, it is coming. You do not have to move forward in your life being defined by the same adjectives you're using today. You were not meant to stay there, and that place does not have any right to have victory over you a single day longer. You are worth so much more.

So where's the way out?

First, you have to be able to answer one question.

WHAT AM I EVEN SEARCHING FOR?

*Shame corrodes the very part of us that
believes we are capable of change.*
—Brené Brown

THERE ARE PROBABLY A LOT of reasons why people choose to raise a family in a small town.

You can buy a house with a big yard and plenty of space. The only time rush hour ever exists is when the county fair is happening once a year. Crime rates are low, there are more opportunities for community involvement, and odds are good your special little town will have some sort of quirky tradition that everyone insists on keeping alive and thriving. Light pollution? You won't find it here. And since there's only about six thousand of you in town, you can go ahead and get to know darn near each and every last neighbor within your ten-mile pocket of paradise.

What's not to love?

My experience with it all reads a little more like the big yard didn't really make up for the small house, especially when non immediate family members needed a place to live. The county fair is great and all, but why do we only get something to do once a year? I unintentionally dedicated myself to increasing the otherwise low crime rates, the community involvement was clearly reserved for the rich, popular, and talented—all descriptors that do not reflect me personally—and if I have to hear one more patron affectionately refer to this place as "the Christmas Card Town" instead of the actual name, I may vomit. A lack of light pollution is just an ever-present reminder that you have to drive forty-five minutes to the closest city with anything open past 9:00 p.m. And as a daughter of one of the only pastors in town, getting to know your neighbors looks a lot more like your dad is the town shrink, and since he's in the business of helping people with their dirt, people are in the business of making sure they magnify every speck of dirt his whole family has and mercilessly judge you for it.

Yeah, what's not to love.

I guess you could say my life didn't exactly mirror what generally comes to mind when you let the warm and fuzzy "small-town charm" picture gently settle into your imagination. Unless you've also renamed the small town you live in "hell." Then, yes, it mirrors it perfectly.

I'm the last of three kids born to a set of very conservative Christian parents. The kind of conservative where I wasn't allowed to wear pants to church (*church*, defined: a mandatory family parade every Sunday morning, Sunday evening, and Wednesday evening, whether you want to or not, every single week) simply because I am female. The kind of conservative that insists on providing a private Christian education, whether it's affordable or not. The kind of conservative where rock music has nothing good to say, so it's better avoided. The kind of conservative where television was monitored because shows like *The Simpsons* advocated kids disrespecting their parents.

They weren't too far off on the last one, but I trust you're starting to get the picture.

The neighborhood I grew up in was a block of four streets, and it was the Midwest, so it was actually laid out on a grid. It was surrounded by a cornfield on one side, a cornfield on the other side, a cornfield in the back, and then a bunch of woods until you got to—you guessed it—a deer farm. The vegetarian in me now cringes when I think back on the fact that I grew up within a mile of what may have very well been a slaughterhouse, or at least their supplier.

School was also very conservative. Fridays were formal days because we had chapel, so all girls in a dress. To this day, I still have no idea how wearing a dress makes you any holier.

On any other day, you could wear a T-shirt, but only if the front collar was double stitched. I remember teachers walking around and inspecting every collar in the class, breaching all sense of personal space, then sending kids out to either get picked up for the day or brought a change of clothes so they could return to class acceptably. Again, if stitches brought us any closer to Jesus Christ himself, the whole charade was lost on me. I remember spending days in fear after realizing I showed up in the garb of sinners with my single stitch, anxiously keeping my head tucked close to my chest to avoid being called out and its subsequent punishment. Second-graders shouldn't have to feel anxious over such trivialities.

But what else would there have been to fuel my ever-growing foundation of awareness of not being good enough down to the most minute detail?

Turns out, plenty.

My class was consistently the largest in the K–12 school, carrying an average of twenty-two kids. You'd think that'd mean there wouldn't be room for social circles with numbers like that, but I'm pretty sure it played out exactly the opposite.

Being born the runt of the litter in my family, I found it hard to make an identity for myself. I was always an expectation before I was just *me*. Being at school just amplified that feeling.

"We can't wait to see what you can do once you're old enough to take the court!" my teachers would tell me on a fairly relentless basis.

My two older siblings excelled at every sport they tried, seemingly effortlessly. My brother even made the local paper. I was expected to be just as good, if not better. After all, look at the genes I carried!

I tried volleyball and almost took out a baby—yes, an infant human being—in the crowd the first time I went to serve the ball. I tried one more sport after that but quickly abandoned it after we got pummeled in our first game. Public humiliation wasn't something I was willing to sign up for if I could avoid it.

I never really seemed to have an interest in a lot of "normal" things. I liked reading and playing in the woods with my best friend. Whenever there was a birthday party or an event that the whole class was called together for outside of school, all the girls always ended up talking about which of the five boys in our class they wanted to date. I was much more concerned about making sure I could beat the boys at whatever game we ended up playing than trying to plan out my entire future with any of them. Somehow that made me a bit of an outcast.

I'd go as far as to say that that word pretty well sums up most of what I felt like for the first two decades of my life: outcast.

I never really seemed to fit in—anywhere. I was an unexpected surprise to my parents, and by time I showed up on the scene at my home life, my two older siblings were already set and good to go without a third wheel. I spent a lot of time by myself growing up, and that felt okay since it was all I had known.

I had three close friends, and given the size of our class, that felt like enough. But even as a kid, I remember feeling like there should be…more.

The feeling didn't start to arise as relentlessly as it did until middle school hit.

*****

I have to break the story line here because there is something that needs to be said.

Public service announcement: Middle and high school are not meant to be "the best years of your life." Anyone telling you otherwise, no matter how good their intentions, is lying to you.

You may certainly remember those years for the rest of your life, you may come out with some fond memories or some lifelong friends, and that's a wonderful, beautiful thing. But to be clear, the time in your life when you're ten to eighteen years old may be *good*, but they will not be *the best*.

If you need to read that again for it to really sink in, go ahead.
I'll wait.
Take your time.

*****

By the time I hit middle school, my family as a whole was start-ing to feel the effects of trying to navigate life under the microscope of being the family of a public figure, at least as much as you could be relative to the size of the town. To put it insultingly lightly, things weren't going well.

Around that time, my older sister ended up moving out before graduating high school for reasons that are hers to share. My older brother ended up following suit not terribly long after that, again, for reasons that are his to share. But I can tell you it wasn't because they were headed for early college or because they had their lives all figured out.

The pressures of private school were making the entire expe-rience unbearable for me. Some teachers hated me before they ever met me simply because of my last name, and they made little to no effort to hide that fact. I dreaded waking up in the mornings, and I was barely through seventh grade.

I asked my mom if I could switch to public school for the upcoming year because I couldn't take it anymore. If that's how reli-gious people treated each other, I not only wanted no part, I wanted to be as far away from it all as humanly possible.

So there I was, about to leave everyone I'd known for my entire life to date, and home was getting empty—quickly. I was navigat-ing something my siblings never went through—the public school social system—and I didn't know a single person going into it all. My class size went from two dozen kids to well over two hundred, and I quickly began to realize I had developed almost no social skills in my thirteen years of life. It was probably the first time I began to feel truly, deeply alone.

What was left at home was a lot of pain, tears, and tension. Relentless tension, the kind that takes root hard before it seeps into every area of your mind, causing it to spill into every area of your life. It affected and infected everyone.

Tensions in my parents' church started to rise around that time as well. Or at least they grew to a point where it was impossible to hide them any longer.

"What's going on with the pastor's family?" "Why can't they get their act together?" "They call themselves Christians when their lives are like this?" People always talk, but in small towns, it's a lot harder to avoid hearing it all.

Why does it always feel like the entire world expects everyone in the pastor's family to be absolutely perfect? Don't they know that we're no different than they are? We're all just human too.

It all just started to hit one after the other, dominoes of destruction that sought to decimate everything in its path—my path.

And now there was extra added pressure from my parents to be the first kid to graduate high school "normally." But I couldn't understand how things like book reports and art projects could even matter at all when everything felt like it was unraveling. And how could I be able to do that when the two who had brains and brawn who went before me couldn't make it?

If I was an accident from the start, how is it even possible to have this much expectation on me from so many outside sources, from every angle?

I didn't know how to handle any of it. I spent my days at school keeping to myself. I was known as the kid who always had their head in a book. It was the only outlet I could come up with to escape trying to be social. I couldn't relate to anyone on almost any level. All the normal basics like movies, music, TV, and sports were all part of a world I either wasn't allowed access to or wasn't talented enough to be part of.

Keep in mind, the internet hasn't existed forever, and I lived part of my life prior to its existence. So it's not like I was a kid who had a smartphone who simply chose not to be informed. There was no access, and I couldn't google anything to try to help.

It didn't take long to quickly become labeled as the weird kid. I spent every day of middle school lunch hiding in the bathroom stalls so I could avoid the cafeteria and subsequent bullying that would follow. Room temperature sandwiches eaten a foot away from a public toilet really don't leave you feeling quite as satisfied as it otherwise may.

I felt trapped in a school that hated me, in a town that looked down on me, in a home that pressured me to fit in with a world it was unwilling to equip me for.

Have you ever felt like that? I wouldn't wish it on my worst enemy.

The summer before high school officially started, I learned that two people from my old school were making the jump to join me in the world of public purgatory. Finally, I had a shred of hope.

The year started off a little smoother than the last one ended, but the honeymoon phase quickly dissolved back into the world I had come to know and hate.

It started again with the whispers as I'd walk by. Then people using the hood on my sweatshirt as a garbage basket in between classes. Actual garbage thrown at me, spitballs, and the name-calling. F——, h——, mother——, b——, a——, c——, freak, r——, the list was colorfully long. There was that fun game that went on and off where people would see who could knock everything out of my hands the fastest as they barged by me.

Most days, it quite literally felt like the entire place was out to cut me down. I don't even understand what I did to any of these strangers. I don't even know most of their first names.

My better inner sense tells me every time, *Just tell someone. Anyone. You have to make it stop.* Everything in me agonizingly entertained the idea like an insect of prey reaching for respite while being bound in its final cocoon, gasping for every last precious breath, knowing the only inevitable outcome ends where you currently lie.

I've tried before.

When I was just a kid in first grade, I had a grade school friend who went to my folks' church, and sometimes my siblings and I would go over to their house for an afternoon. The member of their family who was in my grade wanted to "play a game" with me, which resulted in them putting their hands down my pants.

I hated this game.

It would continue on despite my objections, not only during those times but also at school. One time our class was walking across the building to go to music class, and it happened in line in the hallway while we were waiting for everyone to finish up in the bathrooms. I had hit my limit and ended up yelling at this person to stop. Our teacher scolded me and asked me why I was yelling, to which I replied, "Because she keeps putting her hand down my pants and touching me!" My teacher's face turned red as she fiercely told me lying is a sin and I should be punished for making up these things. At six years old, I indignantly replied, "I am NOT lying!" I was reprimanded again publicly before the class continued on across the building.

That was one of the first times I learned to give up. There a seed was planted, and there its roots grew deep.

How dare you bring to light any abuse or hardship you endure. You shameful monster! the memory taunted.

And because that was my takeaway, that's the scale I think I ended up using as my youth continued.

Well, is what you're going through right now any worse than that thing you literally got publicly humiliated for in your attempt at salvation?

Most things ended up being in the "probably not" category.

So why would this time be any different? This unwanted accident, third wheel, deserved recipient of pain—the things I had learned to identify myself as—told me all too well that trying to stand up for yourself was a privilege reserved for the people who deserved to be here. Not for rejected outcasts like me.

There was too much pain from past failed attempts already weighing me down, feeling like it could crush me at any second. I can't imagine trying to take on more. I feel like I live in a constant state of needing someone else to give me their strength to get to tomorrow. But look at who I'm surrounded with. Where do I turn? Who even *sees* me, let alone would *care* enough to actually help?

What am I searching for? Anything. Anything at all in the slightest that will get me out of my reality even for a moment. Anything to help lighten the burden of shame that was constantly being forced upon me. Anything that could help me forget that I was an unwanted accident. I didn't care what it was. If it could provide me even an hour of respite from life as I know it, I would be sold.

It was around that time that one of the two people I knew at school pulled me aside after class with a proposition, unbeknownst to me then, that would begin to change the next several years of my life.

My friend had managed to befriend one of our class drug dealers, and we had an opportunity to split a bag of weed to try for the first time.

Now if you think it's absurd that a high school freshman would already be experimenting with soft drugs, I feel it's my duty to kindly advise you to go ahead and pull your head out of whatever part of the ground you've chosen to bury it in. By that time, I was already late to the party as far as that scene is concerned. If you're not creating an open dialogue with your kids about these things early on, don't be surprised when you find out they've figured it on their own. We don't live in a Disney movie, and these options are available to everyone.

For years, my family carpooled with another family out to our private school. For years, when we would drop off the other kids, my dad would always say, "Jesus loves you. Don't do drugs!" And for years, that was the only knowledge I had of that entire other world.

But by now, I had already disbelieved the first part of that statement. If Jesus really loved me so much, then why was I an accident? If he really cared, then why was my life like this? Why is every day so hard? Why is it such a seemingly endless struggle to get through even the most basic of moments, like lunch period? Why is my family falling apart? Why am I the somehow apparent enemy of half the town? If he's really a savior, shouldn't he be in the business of saving me from even a single aspect of any of this? Yet here I still am, several years into this mess with several years to go. If you really cared about someone like that, if you really loved them, how could you look down at *this* and do nothing?

I didn't only not believe that by now, but the more I had to hear it, the angrier it would make me. Resentment began to build. If God's love was really true, it was clearly something that was reserved for everyone else but me, just like everything else in my life.

And with that firm resolve in mind, my friend and I set a day and time to delve into one of the last things in this world that still offered any hope to me.

We snuck into her attic after school one day, bag in one hand and our makeshift Mountain Dew can in the other as delivery method of choice. She had also managed to borrow a bit of vodka from a family member, so we polished that off before going upstairs. It was like guzzling straight rubbing alcohol before inhaling something that smelled like it came out of a skunk. I didn't like either of them, and I didn't really feel much different. But our supplier had been sure to tell us these things usually take a few times before you'll really feel anything. And I had nothing else left to hope in, so I figured I might as well just stick with this until I get the real experience.

In the days that followed, for the first time in years, something good actually happened. Because we still had a lot of weed left and because we had split the cost, my friend asked me if I wanted to go to a small party with some of her friends. We would bring what we had, and her friends were going to bring some wine coolers.

Finally, after years of being the outcast, I at last had something that other people wanted, something of myself that I could offer. Finally, I had some common ground.

Why was I told for years and years, "Don't do drugs"? Because right now, drugs are the thing that is bridging the gap for me into normalcy. The only thing in years that actually got me an invite to anything.

That was all the motivation I needed to go ahead and fully disregard the only advice from either of my parents that I ever really got regarding drugs. This is the only thing that's helped me fit in with anyone.

And in that moment, my iron grip on this brand-new world was birthed.

Despite getting sick out of all ends by the time morning rolled in, I considered the party a success. I had made a few more friends who had other friends who eventually led me to my core group of friends I'd have for the rest of high school. Weed had already done more for me than Jesus as far as I could tell, and it only took a couple months.

But there was still an overwhelming black hole of emptiness and soul-gripping depression inside. I thought making a few more friends and finding something that helped distract me from my reality would be enough. But it isn't.

My mind pulls me back to a montage of the hundreds of times anyone's called me a derogatory homophobic slur. If there was one thing my Baptist upbringing taught me, it's that being gay is right up there with adulterers, murderers, pedophiles, and whatever else tops your "worst of the worst" list.

I always found it confusingly contradictory that I was taught "sin is sin," yet we can justify away white lies and "lesser offenders." Shouldn't that, in and of itself, nullify the flat principle that sin is sin? Why is the Bible so confusing? Or is it more that humanity is making it more complicated than it was intended to be?

I literally can't remember a single time in my life where I could ever picture myself with a husband. Heck, I remember always being the one to play the husband in early grade school at recess during games of house. I always thought I was normal until dozens upon dozens of my peers began to tell me otherwise.

The shame started slowly, but once it gained momentum, there wasn't any stopping it. A hatred within myself, for myself, was growing at an alarming rate. And the current amount of allies and escapism I had was not nearly enough to halt the beginning of this impending avalanche.

One of the worst parts about it all is that I can't tell anyone I'm struggling with this. If this is what it's already like without admitting to anything, I could imagine how much worse it'd get on a daily basis if anything was confirmed. I have no idea why this is my burden to bear. This is what heaven's rejects are gifted, I guess.

Even still, I struggle as best I can to suffocate those feelings. They must never see the light of day. *You're already one of the biggest regrets of your parents and your families lives, don't make it any worse for them,* I tell myself.

Over the next couple months, I have one of those standard doctor appointments that you tend to have to progress through high school. I'm convinced there is something chemically wrong with me by this point. Normal people just don't feel like this all the time. I shouldn't be having these thoughts, and I shouldn't be feeling such smothering, deep depression all my waking moments. I remember seeing ads for antidepressants while I'd watch *The Price is Right* over summer break.

Clearly, I am broken. Please, something fix me.

The doctor does a depression screen on me, and, big surprise, I'm a perfect candidate to start on Zoloft. I ask her to talk to my folks about the decision. We're really not a "talk about your feelings" kind of family, and since my brother and sister are already gone, I don't have the spine to tell them to their faces myself.

The shame continues to grow, even when things enter my life that are supposed to be "answers." I am broken, and now it's out in the open for my folks to see. I feel like I let them down, like I've begun to ruin the normal high school career I was supposed to be having.

But I am broken, and I need an outside source to help fix me. The medication that is supposed to help make me normal just makes me feel like I've been branded with a giant scarlet "A." I may not be an adulterer, but the fact that I can't imagine having a husband or kids makes me feel like one. I'm sure I deserve that "A," just like I deserve all the other hardships I encounter.

This is who you are, this is what you deserve, I explain to myself over and over. *This is the life you were born into. This is what accidents get.*

A couple quick months and several doctor appointments later, I find myself on the highest legal dose of antidepressants you can give someone outpatient. But I didn't feel any different. Like, at all. I still had all the same thoughts and feelings I did before, and not a single thing was changing in my day-to-day, that's for sure. How can someone be this messed up?

The shame never stops growing. It's gotten so large, it's almost all I can think about most days, unless I manage to get a little escape from booze or weed here or there. What else is there to be done? Because of where we live, I can't change schools. And the thought of going back to where I used to be at the religious judgment fest makes me want to jump off a bridge.

Inevitably, with pretty much every other scrap and bit of knowledge every parent hopes their child never encounters in their lifetime, the world of self-harm had been introduced to me through various television programs and the public school experience in general.

My mom found out after the first time I needed medical attention because of it, which was maybe four months or so into it. Nothing a few staples couldn't fix. Like everything else up to this point, it started off slowly enough.

It gave me moments in my life where I felt like I could control time; everything else would just fade away. I could be the one to control the pain I felt, for once. It made me feel like I had a way of letting out the cries of my deepest, darkest secrets. It created the facade that I could cast my shame on the outside of me to make it easier to bear inside. But it was a picayune bartering system with the world.

See? I know! I already know what a disappointment I am, so please, just stop, the voice of my dripping shame would plead. But instead of leaving, it would just continue to grow and grow.

It was clear to me by now that this was just how my life was going to be. An endless series of me being a failure, disappointment, sinner, broken, useless, burden. The weight of the shame of who I am and what I've done to try to fix it has broken me. I spend months thinking about ways I can off myself.

One night, I'm alone in my room, crying from the deepest depths of my despair. I throw tissue after tissue at the garbage can across the room as I cry for hours, part out of frustration and part out of deep anger.

I reach the ends of my desperation, and I pray out loud, through tears, still throwing tissues, "God, if you're real, and you actually see me and hear me in the slightest, then show me a sign. Show me anything to tell me that even one person sees me and cares about me." The pile of tissues on the floor has got to be three quarters of the box by now. Like everything else about me, my aim is terrible. "God, if I'm not supposed to kill myself, then let the next tissue make it in the garbage can." My last attempt.

I flippantly toss the last tissue in my hand at the garbage, and I wish I was making this up. It looked as if it was on an invisible perfectly arched track straight from my hand to the can. It looked fake.

I break down again, more confused than angry, still drenched in my despair. It's enough to get me through the night, at least, and probably all the proof I need to believe in heaven. It's challenging to describe it accurately, but it just felt a little too oddly coincidental. So I give it the benefit of the doubt.

I manage a couple more months, but not with ease. It's like there's a constant voice in me whispering *just do it* all the time.

My shame has broken me beyond repair.

Finally, enough is enough.

*****

You already know where I'm going with the story from here.

I would love to be able to sit here and tell you that the next morning, I woke up, confessed to everything, got medical attention, corrected medication, and the therapy I needed to move out of this stage of my life.

But we both know that's not the pretty little bow on top of the neatly wrapped package of teenage angst I ended up with.

Like I said, from this point forward, as far as I can tell, I have basically two options.

And given my logic up to this point in time, you know I didn't go with option one.

I have yet to be able to clearly define what it is I'm searching for. I just know I'm at rock bottom.

Wait, this *is* rock bottom…, right?

It can't get much worse than this…right?

CALL IT WHAT IT IS

In situations of captivity the perpetrator becomes the most powerful person in the life of the victim, and the psychology of the victim is shaped by the actions and beliefs of the perpetrator.
—Judith Lewis Herman

T RENCHES ARE A DANGEROUS PLACE to be; don't be fooled. On the western front, trenches got their beginnings in World War I. For almost four years, between 1914–1918, roughly thirty-five thousand miles of trenches were painstakingly created.[1]

There were a few different methods used to go about this. The easiest but most vulnerable method was called entrenching, where soldiers would simply dig starting at ground level, leaving them exposed to whoever felt like firing at them. The second and much safer method is called sapping, where soldiers would simply continue to extend the trench from the end they were in. The last method was tunneling, which is exactly what you'd think it is. They'd dig a tunnel, then remove the roof last, making them the safest from enemy fire.

There's always more than one way to get yourself to the bottom of a trench. Some ways may look a little easier or draw you in with their false sense of security. But at the end of the day, regardless of your method of choice, the fact remains that you are still stuck in a hole surrounded by thousands of things that are trying to attack you.

Trench life was grueling. The weather itself was one of the first challenges, creating an endless need for repairs from erosion in freezing cold conditions. Sprinkle in nature's mishaps in the form of lice, frogs, rats, et cetera. The lice were so rampant that they gave cause for a disease to be named after their affects called trench fever. So besides the standard itching, added to it were fever, headache, and sore muscles, bones, and joints.[2]

And let's not forget about trench foot. Even though they'd cover the trench floors with wooden boards, aka duckboards, it wasn't enough to fight the elements. The endless cold and constant wet were the start of this disease. It could lead to blisters, ulcers, perma-nent nerve damage, gangrene, amputation, and even death. In fact, trench foot killed at least seventy-seven thousand soldiers before the war was over.[3]

I imagine there were probably an overwhelming majority of people who never believed, out of all the ways their lives could've ended in a war, that a detail as small as wet socks and shoes would be the final stepping stone before meeting their maker.

Trenches aren't there for you to just go and have a fun visit. You're there because there's a war going on all around you. You take refuge because your life depends on it. It messes with your mentality, and in those moments, the trench itself becomes your savior.

Our guards are lulled down with that false sense of security, leaving room for the hidden and insidiously unexpected dangers of the trenches to start their work.

There's a choice all of us have to make either way when we reach those points in our lives. Will you choose to blame the duckboards, or lack thereof, for your case of trench foot, or will you choose to change your socks?

*****

It was another typical day in my senior year of high school. I had started drinking at my standard 6:30 a.m. and casually contin-ued throughout the length of the day, as was now my daily norm.

A shot here and there in the bathroom in between classes. Three or four at lunch. Maybe five or six if I manage to sneak away for a quick smoke before the bell.

Here and there I'd skip eating to allot more time for these "important" things in my day, so by the time I got home, I'd be ravenously hungry.

One day in particular, I threw one of the ever-in-stock $2 frozen pizzas from my parents' freezer in the oven, then decided to take another shot while I was waiting for it to bake. Like most other human beings who go ten hours on an empty stomach while drinking copiously throughout the day, it turned out I had fallen asleep without setting a timer on the food.

I know this because I woke up to my mom pounding on my door, asking why the house was filled with smoke. I manage to tell her I had gotten sick throughout the day and had fallen asleep because of that before apologizing.

She acknowledges how awful I look and accepts it, no questions asked. I apologize again as I go to take out the large black puck my former meal of the day had become. I settle for ramen before I retreat back to my room.

The guilt is eating me alive.

Why do you keep lying about this?

Maybe if you just told anyone else the truth, you'd actually be able to get a little help and stop living like this. Aren't you sick of chugging vodka at 6:30 in the morning just so you have the strength to walk through the front doors of your inhumane four-year sentence insultingly and illegitimately named "high school"?

What I longed for, maybe even needed to hear at that point, was for someone to tell me it was okay that I'd made a lot of mistakes. A mountain-sized load of mistakes, with full intention to make at least one of the same later again that night.

I needed someone to say that it was okay that I was broken. That the world wouldn't shatter if I wasn't everything I was supposed to be, and I could stop cracking under the pressure of failing to be perfect.

I needed to hear that I wasn't unlovable because of the things I've done or because of the feelings I had that drove me to make the decisions that I did. I needed to hear that those things didn't define me, and I didn't have to keep rooting myself in them. I needed to hear not to be afraid of letting go of the familiar in case more bad steps right back in its place. I needed someone to help guide me out of my broken mentality.

I needed more than guidance. I had so many shreds and pieces of myself scattered behind and all around me. How could I ever heal from being an alcohol-drenched, pill-snorting, anything-smoking, self-harming, self-degrading, hopeless core of overwhelming shame and sadness I had become? How could anything ever heal me or make me feel whole?

Could anything like that even exist at this point? I needed to hear someone tell me that I wasn't too far gone. I probably would have laughed in their face, but the deep need in my soul was still there. Longing for forgiveness, longing to be accepted and embraced despite what I had done and walked through.

And I was openly searching for this by now. I was on therapist number five at this point. After four strikes from folks who were definitely not my choosing, I had earned a chance to pick one out myself.

The first try was a couple who were not unfamiliar to me. My former kindergarten teacher—yes, the one who could make me blush at five years old because she looked like a Disney princess in my eyes—and her husband did counseling on the side, and it was somehow in my best interest to give it a go with them. So you know, this is clearly a great idea right off the bat.

We had one session together. My very first experience with therapy at all. I figured everything is confidential, so I may as well just be honest.

I tell them about the medication I'm on, and we go over what to expect on it, side effects, pros and cons. The topic of feeling suicidal naturally arises, and I figure it's all confidential, so I make the decision to be vulnerable and finally tell someone else what I've done. They're the first people I've spoken the words out loud to: "I have tried to kill myself, and failed."

They ask me if I'm still feeling this way now. I can't seem to find the words to give a clear answer. After some back-and-forth, combined with a realization that they may be able to hospitalize me against my will if I can't give them a satisfactory response, I manage to give a clear and stern no to their question of my current state.

The session wraps up, and I get up to leave. But before I can, they pull my mom into the office. I have no idea where they're going with this.

They sit us all down and proceed to tell my mom just about everything I had shared with them. My heart sinks, and the familiar feeling of overwhelming shame drowns me.

I thought this was private? I thought you were supposed to be able to speak in confidence during these things? I had actually believed that maybe I could start to get some help. But now the only thing that's clear is that I can't trust these people. I feel like I just got stabbed in the back.

Not much conversation happens after that other than me drawing the line on going back to them for a second round of broadcasting some of my darkest secrets. All this experience has taught me so far is to keep my guard up at all times.

I don't know where else to turn for relief, so I turn back to what's already familiar to me.

The next year or so is a blur of new therapists and new drugs. And I don't mean prescriptions. I've managed to make friend groups outside the realm of fellow high schoolers. You don't get a seat at the high rollers' table trying to play with dime bags and half pints.

So now between everyone I know, it's pretty easy to get pretty much anything I want.

Cue in my nine-month bender. No, that's not a typo.

For nine straight months, I'm black-out something every single day. There are no longer any breaks in between. Alcohol, weed, valium, Vicodin, Percocet, opium, coke, mushrooms, ecstasy, Adderall—it didn't matter. If it could be found, I was ready to ingest. My weekend job existed solely to fund my escapism.

And when the wells would run dry, I was not above stealing what I thought I needed to help get me through the day. I've no doubt if I sat down and did all the math, the amount I stole has got to be in the thousands. It became second nature. Go to the grocery store, swipe a bottle. Empty a case of beer. Grab a pint at the gas station. Go into the liquor store and swipe a bottle before trying to pay and getting denied because I was four years shy the legal age. How else could I manage to keep what I needed in stock when I'm downing an entire bottle daily?

I finally got caught on a tandem mission I went on with a boy I was trying to impress because I thought he liked me. Turns out, he didn't feel that way.

I don't think I understood what true adrenaline was until I had officers pointing their guns in my face, telling me to freeze. Freezing is very easy to do in that situation.

It was my very first arrest. The first of many, actually. It's a lot harder to learn lessons when you're barely sober enough to know where you even are.

Just a side note: if you're ever in court and the judge asks you if you have anything to say, the correct answer is yes—yes, you do have something to say. Apologize for your stupidity. It'll be better for you if you do.

Anyways, I'm back with another set of married therapists now, after striking out with an über-religious one that was over the Illinois border and another one that made me feel like I was crazy simply because I was a woman. Hard pass.

After a few sessions, they're convinced I'm an alcoholic. I don't argue this conclusion. We talk over various options for me to pursue regarding extended treatment. I'm open to anything that could get me out of going to high school every day, so I take the bait.

They explain to me that by now, if I detox on my own, I'll likely go through severe withdrawal symptoms, which could include seizures and all sorts of other unpleasantries. So they tell me I'll need to go to an emergency room for intake for a proper medical detox. There's no way to avoid telling my mom all this since I'm still a minor, and the all-too-familiar feeling of shame and disgrace fills me once again.

A few days later, my mom and I head to the only ER in town. Despite being the only ones there, we find ourselves waiting for an hour that no doubt feels like an eternity. So many thoughts come in and out of my mind.

What will it be like? Will any of the complications take me before the detox process is over? Where will I go after this? How long will I be there? When will I finish school? How will I manage to keep my friends if I have to be sober? Who even am I when I'm sober?

Finally, a nurse comes out to us with my paperwork. She looks over it and tries to clarify why we're there. My mom does all the talking, and the look on the nurse's face never reflects anything besides confusion.

We're on the same page after about fifteen minutes. I don't know if it's because of my age, but the nurse told us they wouldn't take me. I feel like she doesn't believe us or thinks details are being embellished.

Why do people in authority always think I'm lying when I finally have the courage to come to them for help? Why would anyone lie about this? I just don't understand. Why do I even keep trying?

I never make it past the waiting room. She just tells us to go home and keep seeing my therapist. So we leave.

I go back to see the married couple again and tell them what happened. They start giving me a mountain of information on places for me to pursue for long-term treatment. My mind glazes over not long into the conversation.

A lifetime of being the poor kid is all I need to know to conclude there's no way any of these places are going to happen. We don't even pay rent (church parsonage perks), and my dad still works three jobs. I decide this is the last time I need to see these two. If this is their last resort option to give me, there's nothing left here.

I go back to what I know again, really hard into the stimulants this time. Adderall and I are besties. I end up losing about fifty pounds in four weeks or so. I'm awake for two to four days at a time, with the energy of a superhero and the appetite of someone on chemo. I don't think anyone's noticed the change in me. It's not like I got new clothes or anything to show it off. And it's not like anyone's that invested in me personally to ask any questions about it.

Some friends and I take a day trip up to Madison. I'm on somewhere between 120–150mg of Adderall, and we're smoking the whole way up to the city. I start slipping in and out of consciousness. My heart has never felt like this before. It's got to be beating faster than a hummingbird's wings. My chest and arm start to hurt. I wonder to myself if I'm having a legitimate heart attack. We finally get there, and the next thing I know it's already tomorrow afternoon. I wonder to myself, *What happened?*

I check my wrist for a hospital band, check my wallet and car for any clues, but find nothing other than an empty bottle and low supply of drugs. By now a morning without surprise police reports from the day before, I consider a success. So naturally, I celebrate by going right back at it again.

I'm on my fifth therapist now, the one I got to pick. Her office is in the city downtown and about an hour drive one way. Like just about everything else in this small town, all it does is make you feel like you're a million miles from getting out or from any help.

But I actually start to not even mind the drive. It makes me feel like I can catch my breath for a minute, being able to put some distance between me and the place that's slowly killing me.

And it turns out I actually really like her. She doesn't put pressure on me like everyone else before her had. She doesn't try to cram religion down my throat before each session is over. If I can't find the words to say, which is often, she doesn't just sit in silence until I come up with something. She actually tries to help me figure it out. For maybe the first time, I start to feel like I might actually have an ally. Albeit one that requires payment, but an ally nonetheless.

The better part of the year starts to go by. Talking with her is easier than most, but talking in general is still quite a challenge for me. At school, I'm almost mute, speaking only in class when it's required of me, but that's about it.

I've learned the easiest way to deal with bullies is to simply look them dead in the eye after their insults, say nothing, and try best I can to continue on with my day. It's seemed to help. It's hard to tell if I've solved this problem or simply become fully apathetic toward their efforts. I just can't find the energy to care about them anymore. It's strength beyond me.

I begin to finally become a mystery to most of the world around me, and people finally seem to begin to start losing interest in using me as their punching bag. But it's challenging to just turn the silence on and off, so I just tend not to speak.

I can almost feel like I don't even exist after a few days like this. Like I'm living outside of myself, watching my life from an audience instead of seeing it all from behind my own eyes. It's harder to relate to people now. Everyone seems to have something they care about. What do I have? I don't even care anymore how anyone treats me. I guess I have drugs. At least that's something.

Am I the only one who feels like this?

All this has made my therapist's job exceedingly difficult, since she's not an actual mind reader. She does her best to continue to encourage me to get out of there as soon as I can after graduation. I need to move to the city, where there are more people like me, or just more people in general. I need to be able to "be who I really am," something that won't be able to happen where I live now.

I don't disagree, but how am I going to make that happen working a minimum wage job? The thought of leaving this place is the first time I've felt some form of hope in years, but even if I quit everything I use for comfort and devote every last dollar to getting out, the feat still seems wholly unattainable.

I feel sunk before I even begin. How does anyone pull this off? Discouragement begins to smother what little hope I allowed myself to feel. And the weight of it all makes my chest heavy and my mind and mouth slow to move.

I feel like I can't do it. Like I'll be stuck where I am for the rest of however long my life is. I can't break the ever-on-repeat voice in my head that tells me I'm going to fail at this, just like everything else in my life. I thought if I just had one person in my life who believed in me, that would be enough. But I can't seem to make her voice louder than the voices of all my past defeats.

It gets harder and harder to talk to her. I feel like I'm letting down one of the only true allies I have, and the shame starts taking over me like so many countless times before. It's easier not to speak than to admit out loud what a failure I endlessly seem to be.

Eventually we come to our last session together. It's her decision, not mine. She tearfully tells me that she doesn't think she's helping me anymore, that I don't seem to be making any more progress.

I nod in agreement. I may be silent, but I'm not blind. And she's right, there's no reason for me to be a burden on her any longer. I imagine there are so many other people in my life who wish they could just dump me. I envy the relief she must feel.

I'm done with therapy now. I'm done with medications. I'm done trying to find things that I think will help me be a "normal" person. I just don't have the energy anymore to try even one more time. I get it. I know what I am. What I have been is what I always will be—a failure and a disappointment.

Senior year is coming to a close now, and somehow I've managed to graduate just fine. I find it insulting that you can be drunk or drugged out of your mind for nine months straight and still have the ability to graduate with upward of a 3.0 GPA. What exactly are they trying to teach me here? What was the point of all those years of misery?

Barely three months out of graduation, I find myself on yet another bender.

It's unusually cold this September, even for Wisconsin. A buddy and I managed to get a bottle for the day but decide to call it an early night because of the cold. I get in the car to start driving us less than two miles home since I'm still one of the only one of us who has a license. Town is deserted since it's past eight o'clock, one of the only downsides-now-turned-perk for me.

We come to a two-way stop, and I look left and right. All clear. I let off the brake, and in that moment, life turned into slow motion.

I look left and see a motorcycle. I'm in his path, and he doesn't have a stop sign. I know what I have to do is hit the brake hard and throw it in reverse, but there's not enough time. I feel my heart beat. I feel like I'm watching a movie. My heart beats louder and faster. There's just not enough time. *Buh bump, buh bump, buh bump, bump, bump.*

He slams into the driver engine side of my car and flies over the hood on his stomach. I debate running, but I know the car is in my parents' name. It'll come back to me no matter what I do. I get out to see if he's all right. Thankfully, he was wearing a helmet and going the posted speed limit of twenty-five miles per hour.

It must've been louder than I thought. Patrons from the local bar start pouring out to see what happened as the police roll up.

The officer takes me to the sidewalk to perform some field sobriety tests. I notice the large six-foot electrical box placed to the left of the stop sign I failed to stay stopped at long enough. The motorcycle must have been behind it in the second I checked to my left. I try to explain that to the officer, but he obviously has no interest in my reasoning as to why he's here.

I fail all the tests with flying colors, so they book me and take me to the station for a Breathalyzer. I blow a 0.27 before literally passing out and falling over. Looks like I won't be talking my way out of this one.

I lose my license, receive upward of $1,000 in fines since I also had all sorts of paraphernalia on me, and am ordered to take some sort of class to go along with my many hours of community service. The OWI will stay on my record for ten years. I suppose simple theft and multiple counts of possession were getting lonely on my record all by themselves. At least I avoided jail.

Can this please just be rock bottom already?

I don't know if you've ever tried to bike to work in two feet of snow every day, but let me just tell you, it's worse than it sounds. And did that help me learn my lesson?

Let's just say it's hard to gain a proper takeaway when you loathe the outside sources keeping you stuck as much as you loathe yourself. I'm not exactly a shining example of someone reformed by the judicial system.

The winter passes, as do my fines and punishments. In the spring, a good friend from school asks if I want to move to the city and get a place together. She's going to college but is trying to get an apartment off campus to save some money.

I have no money saved up since my fines took all I had. I have no job lined up in the city. I have almost nothing going for me. But I know I have to get out. It's time to stop skirting the truth. It's time to face what I really am. I am an addict. And I know if I stay here, it's all I'll ever be.

And if I move, I'll finally be able to stop going to church for good. Much like my first school, all that place had to offer me was judgment, condemnation, and impossibly high standards to meet.

So I'm sold. We work out the details, and the move happens within a couple of months. The fresh start I've been waiting years for is finally here.

I find employment fairly quickly upon moving. One gig in retail and another as a bartender at a local music venue. I'm a nineteen-year-old kid with a mohawk, selling things that make drinking fun or getting paid to drink on the job while listening to some of my favorite bands.

I feel accomplished.

It's finally starting to feel like I can do this. But even though I've moved, new connections opened right up, almost without trying. "Go clean the bathroom" doesn't mean what you'd think it means. My retail boss occasionally leaves lines for me on the back of the toilet at work to make our shifts together more fun.

I've progressed from being the messed-up weirdo outcast to being the punk who never turns down a party. All my bullies are gone, and I think I'm finally starting to have some self-esteem. I'm dating my first love, and I start to believe I might actually be able to pull it off. I might actually be able to be…happy.

Maybe this whole time, what all my habits were actually doing was masking one of the only things I was desperately searching for all along—happiness.

It's strange what your brain fills in for you when you're not paying attention. How it can keep giving you the same answer even though you're asking a different question, and how easily we continue to accept its answers simply because it's become a habit.

I feel like my life is finally starting to fall into place. I'm starting to believe I might have a shot at living past twenty-five years old. New people are coming in, and I feel like maybe I really can leave my former lifestyle behind somehow. At least I finally have a desire in me to genuinely entertain the notion. Maybe my therapist was right, and moving out was what really needed to happen for me to have a real shot at it all.

But the drugs are still very present. Even when I try to avoid them, they find a way to come into my life for free. Frankly, it's hard to turn down "free" anything, especially if it's something I already know I enjoy.

I know it's still something I have to address. But even outside of that, work, relationships, and everything else, I still feel like I'm missing *something*.

Why doesn't this feeling ever go away? I can definitely say I've tried just about everything on earth, everything within my power to try to fill this…void. And my life is finally going well.

So why do I feel like my life is still missing something?

IT'S A SETUP

*The cords of death entangled me, the anguish of the
grave came over me; I was overcome by distress and
sorrow…when I was brought low, he saved me.*
—David

WALTER HARE OF THE WEST Yorkshire Regiment first went into
the front line in December 1916. He describes his experience
as follows:

> We moved to the right, I remember, got into
> a church yard—a cemetery—and then dropped
> down into a trench. And I couldn't believe it; I
> was knee deep in mud for a start. I'd never been
> told about the Somme and the mud on the
> Somme, it was all new to me. Well we sloshed
> down this communication trench and we passed
> a support line and then we went further up and
> got to what was the front line. And then that
> was the first we knew about trench warfare—
> we were told we hadn't to show our heads above
> the parapet because there were snipers and they
> would get us if we did, so we had to be careful.
> It was a bit of a shock because I could hear shells
> exploding and rifles and machine guns going,

and I thought, 'Well, I shan't be here above five minutes.' It depressed you a bit; just I'd not been warned about it, I'd no idea what it was like.[4]

Have you ever been caught off guard by something that ended up changing the trajectory of your entire life?

Okay, you've managed to navigate your trench all right up to this point for as long as you have. You're still alive, right? You're here reading this. So, at least up to this point, you've been making it.

But what do you do when you thought you only had one more turn to go before exit, only to discover that turn ends up leading you to the front line? And now there's a new enemy right in your face with force set to kill and eyes locked on you. What do you do?

One thing you can bank on as sure as the sun will rise is that there will always be a point, after you're in it long enough, that something will catch you by surprise. A surprise that will alter the core of who you are.

You see, the longer you choose to stay in the trenches, the more time the enemy has to think of new and horrific ways to try to destroy you. The more desperate the situation becomes, the more ruthless new tactics become. This is war after all. Don't lose sight of that fact. Just because your little trench has been made comfy cozy down there does not mean it's home. It does not mean it's safe. It does not mean it was meant for you. You have to fight. You have to get out.

Look at what can happen if you don't.

Trench life lead to the first ever use of poison gas in 1915. No progress was being made in the war, and all sides refused to surrender their trenches. And because of that, new evil was birthed.

And more than one new evil. Tanks made their first ever appearance in 1916. Tactics and machinery that are still used to this day were born in the season of trench life. In fact, the *Encyclopedia Britannica* has even more to add to that note.

Some 100 years on, the mass slaughter along the Western Front serves as a brutal reminder of the horrors of trench warfare. Drone warfare, artillery, laser-guided missiles and other technologies have seen military powers in recent times fight battles from a distance. In essence, trench warfare has redefined battle in the modern age.[5]

Did you catch that? Your trench can and will redefine your future. The matter of how you let it change who you are is entirely *your* choice. Part of your job in the trench is to keep your perspective clear and your end goals loud.

> Because the goal of trench warfare was to defend one's own trench while attempting to take the enemy's at the same time, neither side gained any ground in a short period of time. Even if one side did push forward, it would take months at a time to gain anything.[6]

You won't move forward if you choose to continue to try to defend your trench. Months will go by time after time, and what you'll have to show for it is a tired, weary, depleted stalemate.

Your enemy won't just throw in the towel and surrender because they see you in this state, even if you stumbled up to the front line unknowingly. Actually, expect that point to be when the attacks will come in harder than ever before.

And you already know this is true. That's why we have idioms like "kick him when he's down" or "throw salt in the wound." At times, we've already come to expect it to get harder when we're already staring a struggle dead in the eye. That's part of what it's like living in a trench. You anticipate that hardship. It's what you do in the anticipation that's your key.

Our buddy Walter could have realized the situation he was in, let his depression take over him, and easily given his life over to the hands of his enemies. But he knew what we all need to know. That trench wasn't his home.

And even though the attacks of his enemy caught him off guard, even though he had no warning for the levels of shock, dismay, and terror I've no doubt dwelled within him, his ability to push that aside and maintain focus on the facts is surely part of what helped him live through that to tell the story.

When you choose to surrender to and defend what destroys you, what comes out of that is only ever more destruction. But when you choose to let the larger picture come into focus, when you choose to see and believe that restoration will come, the battle won't last forever, that's when the walls of your trench will start to feel smaller than they used to.

Will that be easy? Will that come as second nature? No! This is a battle after all. You have to fight for it. But it is worth the fight, it is possible, and you can do it.

Just not alone.

*****

I've been in the city for a few years now and am living with my second roommate in a new apartment. It'd be nice to say that was all the time I needed to get the rest of my act together. But there's no point in lying to you now. We're too close now, you and I, to waste time playing games like that. And I value our relationship too much to do you dirty.

Things have been progressing though. I think maybe I'm getting close to the top of my trench? Or maybe I've at least gone up a few levels closer to daylight.

I left my bartending gig behind and worked hard to get promoted a couple times in my retail gig. This is success, right? Work your way up a corporate ladder, make more money, earn a grander title. 'Merica, right? This is what we do.

My former manager ended up leaving, and I worked into her role. Well, "leaving" if you mean she didn't show up to work or answer her phone after letting me know she was on quite the bender mixing all sorts of who knows what with oh-so-much booze. We ended up making a wellness call on her behalf, which really ended up saving her life for the time being there.

That's the thing about using what you find when you're down there in the trenches. You know, those things that deceptively look like they might be there to help you. Sometimes those things are people. And sometimes those people come with their own trench and an idea to build connecting tunnels to yours. The mentality that getting out isn't the goal, but expansion.

Those tunnel connectors never show up as shovels but are often disguised as things, in this case, like Percocets and oxys. And they feel good! So it must be the right move on the right path because it feels good right now.

And if you've justified anything in this manner before, that's enough to make it that much easier next time, and next time, and before you know it, you don't even need a justification process anymore to keep making your terrible decisions. It's familiar and normal and comfortable now on your four hundredth time around this circle.

And that's how the idea of expansion even works its way in to your trench life. You've gone around the same circle so many times you've created significant depth in the tread. And now the little "rut" you've been stuck in is an expansive new addition of your "home."

Now you're looking for something to help you out of your new depths, so you invite in this shiny new thing you found down there, and the cycle continues.

I can see it in her because I see it in me. I selfishly hope there will still be more Percs and oxys for me when this particular ordeal is over. Maybe I'm not as close to being out as I thought.

It's my twenty-second birthday, which really is a miracle in and of itself. My folks take me out for a meal on them at a restaurant of my choice. It's then I learn it's been finalized, and they'll be moving a little over six hundred miles away back to where they grew up so my dad can be a pastor at his home church out there instead of the one that helped destroy me out here. Cool. Happy birthday. Thanks.

A couple months later, we're at the house I grew up in, packing up a moving truck, getting ready to say goodbye forever to the town I grew up in. I don't really feel sad or angry about all this. More like scared and fearful. I'm an adult by age, but I still rely on my folks for financial boosts and car help (I've literally had all the car problems. All of them. It's its own novel which I'll spare you, but know it's weighty enough for a valid cause for concern on my end).

My brother joins in the caravan, and we drive twelve hours away to settle them in to their new home. We get there and start unloading, and these three strangers show up, two old ladies and someone a bit younger than my folks. They said they're from my dad's new church, and they came with a ton of food and drinks and…encouragement? This is really weird.

I'm sweaty, full of all sorts of heavy emotion, and really not in the mood to be introduced to the next round of judgments and condemnations at this point. Not interested, please go away now.

One of the older ladies insists on being positive and happy as all heck, and she tries to give me a hug. I refuse, for obvious reasons, and tell her, "No, thank you, I'm quite sweaty and unshowered and just spent twelve hours in a car." And this lady just hugs me anyways. What the actual? I'm not sure how to feel about this. It actually seems deeply genuine. This is strange and unfamiliar territory.

My brother and I spend a couple days there before flying back to the Midwest. I'm filled with far more emotion than I anticipated on the plane ride home.

Justified or not, a large part of me feels abandoned. My folks and what little extended family I have are all six hundred miles away. My sister is now settled over three hundred miles away the opposite direction. My brother is about to get married and graduate college, and they've decided they'll be joining the rest of our family in Pittsburgh too. So it'll be just me.

Like, really just me. My second roommate spent the better part of a year struggling to find employment. Our lease end was coming up just a couple months after my folks' move, and he was at a point where he had to move back in with his own folks for financial reasons. And my first roommate and I aren't on speaking terms any longer.

I have been properly climbing the corporate ladder, and I was offered an actual management position that should actually be able to pay all my expenses without having to rely on anyone else. Finally.

But is this what I even wanted for my life? Whether I wanted to or not, it was time for some actual genuine reflection and decision-making.

Do I really want to work in retail for the rest of my life? Sure, I'm good at it, but do I even *want* it? If I take this position and get a place by myself, that's exactly the life I'll be living for quite many of the upcoming years. Should I even stay in Milwaukee? I'll be the only one left. And no, I certainly have not kicked the booze and soft drugs yet. Most of the hard drugs are gone now though, so at least I'm progressing.

I spend some time toying with the idea of higher education. I'm not excited about the concept of willingly going to school, a notion that still harbors a good deal of pain and resentment in me still. But I am keen on the idea of maybe possibly getting a job I actually want to do and have real interest in.

I float the idea by my mom of moving into their basement bedroom so I can go to college. The timing of it all does make it feel like this might be the best decision for me.

A short while later, she gets back to me with enthusiasm on the idea, but with one condition. If I make the move out there, the trade-off for free housing is contingent on me going back to church.

I feel angry for so many reasons.

I'm angry at the situation itself, angry at my parents for leaving and still trying to cram religion down my throat from six hundred miles away, angry at religion for being the hinge of contingency here, and angry at God.

Isn't he supposed to be up there watching everyone all the time? Hasn't he seen the hell I've already managed to survive? What kind of a sick joke is this? Truly. What kind of depraved masochist would endorse this kind of a setup? I've learned everything I need to learn from religion, thanks very much. I thought I might be getting to the top of my trench, and now there's an actual option for me to start at the very beginning of it all again with religious judgment fest? This is—look, I'm trying not to swear. This is jacked, on every level of its definition.

So what are my options? I stay here in Milwaukee and struggle—alone. Or I uproot everything I've ever known and move to a place I've been once, knowing I'll have to let religion back into my life.

That thought makes me feel like I'd be freeing a serial killer. It feels insane, and it makes me sick.

The idea of walking back through any church doors just brings back all the shame I've worked so hard to subdue. All the anger I can otherwise quiet in my mind roars in and cuts through everything else when I think about religion.

Church defined me, then rejected me, and made me realize what a terrible creature I am. Religion belittled, ostracized, crippled, and, quite literally, almost killed me.

How am I seriously even spending any real time considering this?

I let anger win for the day and hit my trusty methods of escapism. The bottle never judges me, unlike the church.

I find it hard to gain clarity in the days and weeks that follow. I feel like I'm back in a place of seeing my life happen in front of me through someone else's eyes. I try to reason the situation out so I can come to the logical conclusion.

I've actually done a pretty terrible job of making friends so far as an adult. For the most part, if you aren't selling something or into a late night out at the bar or club, you're not someone I have time for. Turns out that's a very niche category to live in. It's quite lonely actually.

But if I stay, I'll be gaining a new role, so I'll naturally have the opportunity to meet a lot more people. But as a manager. How many people hang out with their boss?

Maybe the idea of a fresh start is actually starting to sound appealing to me. Maybe this really is the only way to truly get some sobriety in my life, just up and leave it all behind.

But moving six hundred miles away when pretty much all you know is your parents is legitimately crazy, right? If I had to pick one word to describe my relationship with my dad at this point, it would be nonexistent. And let's face it, deep down maybe I blame him for a lot of my time in my trench. If I just had a normal father with a normal job, or a normal dad that just walked out on his family, then my life would have looked completely different.

I wouldn't be covered in scars, I wouldn't be addicted to, well, everything. If church wouldn't have been such a large part of so much that I knew, I might actually just be a normal adult who could wear shorts and a T-shirt in the summer.

Why. On. Earth. Would anyone ever choose to go back into that if they had the option not to?

Why can't I get that old lady who hugged me out of my mind? I swear, she's haunting my dreams.

And I know I'm still living a lifestyle that isn't sustainable for people who see their forties and beyond.

I'm just at such a loss for the right answer here.

For the first time in years, many, many years, I find myself considering probably the last resort I have. It's incredibly difficult—maybe even impossible—for me at this point to rid myself of the flippant, possibly mocking, certainly disrespectful overtone, but I manage to say the words with the *slightest* drop of genuineness. "Lord, show me what to do," I prayed.

I prayed.

Weird.

I don't even know what kind of an answer I'm expecting. Some cryptic severed hand writing with blood on my wall?

I feel stupid.

Then I feel straight up indignant. "Let's get serious here, God. If you're real, if you hear me, if you care even the slightest ounce about what happens to me in this garbage life you've thrown at me, then I want an answer. Clearly, I care very little what actually happens to me down here. But if you're anything like everyone says you're cracked up to be, then act like it. Show me what to do."

I feel like I'm breaking some or several religious laws by being openly angry at the alleged Creator of the universe. But if you'd walked through life like I have up to this point, you'd be just as angry too.

Then my phone rang.

Just my mom checking in. It has been a few weeks since we talked about me moving, and she just wanted to know if I'd made a decision yet.

I laugh and think about all the places I've looked at in Milwaukee and feel discouraged by the average price of a roof over my head and the average balance of my checking account. After a pack a day, a bottle a day, and any extra, there's little left for things like food and shelter.

I tell her no decision yet. She brings up church again and mentions those old ladies who were there the day they moved in. She tells me they're excited at the thought of me being out there.

Why are these old ladies haunting me? Ugh.

She goes on to talk up the basement quarters and entices me with images of free dinners on a regular basis. Honestly, that thought never crossed my mind yet, and for someone on food stamps, it's kind of a big deal.

We end the call, and I feel a little shook by it all. That was really weird timing, eh? That couldn't have been…an answer? Was that an answer? Is that how this all works? Was that my cryptic severed hand?

The thought of being an adult who moves *back in* with their parents makes me feel like I've already failed. But that is a feeling I'm very familiar with. I think I can actually handle that one this time around.

That old lady. Maybe—I know it's a long shot, but just maybe—*haunting* wasn't the right word. Maybe she was there as some sort of signal that this church would be different.

But why should I even consider giving any church any benefit of any doubt after *everything*? You know what?

Screw it. I'm flipping a coin.

"Show me what to do," I say again.

I wish I could cut to a commercial break or something right here to build suspense.

But this is a book.

So it was heads. I'm moving.

I put in a two-month notice at my job. They tell me I can transfer to a store out there, which was really nice. But I figure if I'm going to start fresh, I may as well just really start as fresh as I can.

I look into renting a moving truck. Turns out it's mad expensive to go across multiple state lines and tow your car behind you. It's so expensive that it would actually be cheaper for me to leave everything I own besides my clothes, my cat, and my car and just buy everything new once I move.

I wasn't expecting this new start to be quite *that* fresh. But the ball's already rolling, no turning back now.

The morning of the move comes quicker than I wanted it to. I can't believe I'm doing this. I've made a mistake.

I'm loading up the last of my belongings into my car at 3:00 a.m. to get ready to drive for twelve hours and over six hundred miles away from everything I have ever known in life. Insane people do this.

"What am I doing?" I say out loud in the parking lot of my apartment building.

Pop!

What the holy heck was that? Did a gun just go off? Why was that so close to me? I am alone at 3:00 a.m. and also an unarmed woman.

There's a cargo van parked three spots away from my car. A very lean and muscular guy walks quickly and very closely past me and swears under his breath. It dawns on me the pop was a tire getting slashed. I know the van belongs to my neighbors who are either very much on or very much selling heroin. Likely both. The police were no strangers to my building. And apparently they've made enemies. With knives.

I freaking panic. I run back upstairs and grab my cat, abandon anything else I might have missed, and get the crap out of there. I'm not about to be the only witness-turned-stabbing victim. Not how this fresh start is going down.

I do, however, pull out my trusty flip phone and give a quick call to the police. Which is weird, because I've never been on the "justice" side with the cops, just the receiving end of "justice." This really is a new start already.

I get about forty-five minutes into the journey and make the first stop in the town we grew up in. I'm meeting my brother there because he's offered to make the drive with me, which I'm thankful for. And I can't think of a more appropriate place to be the starting point at which I leave the Midwest for good.

We get in the car and then it hits me.

I don't know how to get to Pennsylvania from Wisconsin. I didn't even print off a map! I didn't even look one time on what roads to take! (Remember, I'm a '90s kid. I existed slightly before smart-phones and GPS.) I just assumed my brother knew because he's older than me, and, I don't know, he's my brother, so he knows things.

This just went from feeling insane to actually being insane. What. Is. My life.

My brother just motions forward and tells me we'll get there.

It was a very long twelve hours. It's August, so it's hot. And the car I currently have has an oil-burning issue. So I have to stop about every seventy-five to a hundred miles and add a quart of oil to it. To the burning hot engine. In August. I end up going through six bottles of oil, which they sell at 300 percent above normal price at the interstate pit stops.

Is this really the way I'm supposed to take to get out of my trench? This is only day one, and I'm just trying not to get stabbed or get my car towed for hundreds of miles. Maybe I read the signs wrong. I guess I'll find out in time.

Somehow we manage to get there. It takes me all of ten minutes to unload my car. I don't really know what I was expecting to feel in this moment. The amount of sweat my body has produced in this last half of a day is overshadowing the heavy emotions I can feel lurking underneath. The fear, potential regret, panic and anxiousness, loneliness. Yeah, they're all down there.

All the emotions.

I just uprooted my entire life. By my own choice. And Sunday is in just a couple days.

Church.

Ugh.

What have I done.

WHAT YOU CAN CONTROL

When you make completely erasing the memory and existence of hurt and pain your goal, you will be forever chasing an impossible end goal which will cause more mental distress, frustration, and guilt. Rather, focus on making the hurt a part of your beautiful life story.
—Dr. Caroline Leaf

N O-MAN'S-LAND. THE SPACE IN BETWEEN. The unclaimed territory between the front line of your trench and the front line of your enemy. Vast nothingness that exists to hold the tensions of life and death itself.

Sometimes they would lie barren. Other times you would find them littered with abandoned military equipment, barbed wire, and remnants of what felt like a never-ending battle.

The place you were most likely to die, even more so than your trench. The place that turned you from a soldier into nothing more than a sitting duck taunting your opponent with the satisfaction of an easy kill.

Can you see it?

Dense, heavy mud between craters in the earth created from round after round of enemy tank fire. Each step a labored fear-filled struggle of mind and body. Dormant water, rock, ammunition shells, land mines. Oh, the smell, the smell of rotting flesh, unending, unforgiving. Full knowledge that each shallow, strained breath might be your last at any given second.

A designated space to exploit vulnerabilities, the epitome of hell on earth.

No-man's-land.

The late poet Wilfred Owen said it was "like the face of the moon, chaotic, crater-ridden, uninhabitable, awful, the abode of madness."[7]

The abode of madness.

You'd have to be in a pretty desperate situation to poke your head up high enough out of your trench to see that treachery and still choose to walk out into it.

Oftentimes it was between choosing to take that land or waiting for an enemy raid, which would force you into it, anyways.

Either way, for many, facing no-man's-land was facing the beginning of the end.

*****

I'm blindsided by the fact that there is such a dramatic culture shock. I mean, it's the same country, still the US. Just a few hundred miles away in a different time zone. I can't make sense of the fact that there's such a dramatic shift. I've never had so many strangers start talking to me when I've just been going about my daily life. It's weird, and I struggle to understand the accents.

That and the hills. I was not expecting to get motion sick to and from my ten-minute drive to Walmart for the first solid two months of living in Pennsylvania. My ears pop while going down some of the bigger hills the same way they pop when I've flown in a plane. Why didn't any of this happen in the few days I was here when I moved my folks out?

The transition is proving harder than I imagined.

Or I guess it's showing me what I failed to imagine. Which is an interesting notion. What if I've failed to imagine more than just a few additional side effects. What if I've failed to imagine...good?

This all might be helping me consciously realize I've closed the door on the idea that good things can actually happen to me in my life. I've spent so very long believing I don't deserve anything good to happen to me. Maybe it's because I'm in my twenties and kind of an adult now, or maybe it's the fresh perspective sliding in that comes with such a large life change, but I think I actually do deserve some good in my life. I mean, doesn't everyone? And don't I count as an everyone?

That thought gets stuck in me, but in kind of a good way. It helps me see things differently, to see the good in a given situation. This total new way of thinking is really shaking things up. And I kind of really like it. Maybe I really don't deserve to be miserable for my entire existence.

And it pains me to admit this next bit. Which is laughable, given all you've already read through up to this point.

Sigh.

But I'd be lying if I said I hated this new church that's been forced into my life.

I know, I know.

Don't get me wrong—it's not like it's my new favorite thing. Sitting in a pew, staring at a scene that is painfully familiar to me despite not having seen it the past six years. It boggles my mind that a theme of hymn books and a single piano player still lasts, apparently all over the country, to this day. Why do people find this appealing?

At least in this eighty-some odd-person congregation, there are some people who can actually sing. I suppose it's better than the last church? I don't really know how to judge this place. All I know is six years was not long enough for me to get unsick of hearing my dad's preaching style that has definitely not changed one iota since my last appearance.

Talk about motivation to get a plan in place so I can move out of my parents' house—again.

Those old ladies are here. And they said hello and hugged me and seemed genuinely happy that I was here. Like they said they would.

And it still all feels sincere.

My mind can't comprehend this yet. And I refuse to take the bait of encouragement if it's just another show.

If there's one thing I've learned, it's that true colors will always come through. Church is just a place to play charades and act holy and make you feel bad about yourself because you're not that. I get it. I've played this game for a long, long time. And my guard is up.

I've been informed that I have indeed entered Steeler country. Apparently, what that means is when there's sports happening on Sunday, there's extra effort to end the service on time. Apparently, I like sports now because of this fact.

I still don't get what all the hype about religion is if we're just checking off a box on Sundays and getting out as quickly as we politely can so we can get off to our treasured entertainment.

What am I missing here?

I've decided I'm going to pursue gaining education at a local community college. If I'm diving back into allowing religion in my life, I figure I might as well double down with education. But not the kind of education that requires any sort of loan. The whole experience of school in general has already left enough of a mark in my life up to this point. Debt will not be joining that baggage.

The world of breaking news has caught my attention. Maybe it's the adrenaline junkie in me, or maybe the idea of being able to be close to crimes without having to personally commit them is what pulls me in. Either way, I have a hunger in me to drive those mobile news vans and be the first to see and capture what will later be broadcast to the world. It sounds exciting, and I wouldn't mind getting paid for that.

And I feel I've already had every traditional college experience everyone goes away to college for. I definitely couldn't tell you how many basement parties I've been to in my life. Enough of them, that's certain.

Definitely already had plenty of experiences of party bowls of "What pill is this?" "You'll know about forty minutes after you take it," keggers, ragers, making out with random people, running from the cops—yep. Checked it all off my list and more, all before graduating high school.

So I guess I really am just interested in gaining education. Is this what it's like for normal people when they enroll in college? Simply going to get your money's worth and not going for the parties? It's such a foreign feeling.

In an effort to really get my adulting game strong, I go for a job at a local chain restaurant. I have no cooking or kitchen skills. I literally survived on Hot Pockets for more than one year. Adults cook. So I might as well get paid to learn how to do that.

So here we go! Look at this, I'm doin' it! This is the life of someone who has their act together, minus my living situation. Early twenties, juggling full-time work, school, and weekly religion. I don't know why I thought it would be so much harder than it was to get here. This is doable.

It takes me a little over a year to realize that the job I'm working toward is a job of guaranteed nights, weekends, and holidays work schedule. I know I live with my folks, but going for something that ensures I won't see any of my family on any major celebratory day for at least five to seven years just feels kind of foolish. I guess this is one of the reasons people go to school for an education they never end up using. I'm glad I didn't take any loans out for this disappointment.

One of my professors actually owns his own business making local TV commercials. One day while I'm at work perfecting my burrito-rolling skills, I get a voicemail out of the blue from him offering me a paying gig with his company.

I call him back on my break to laugh in his face and tell him I'm happier making minimum wage at a restaurant.

I'm kidding! I took the job, like a sane person. But it starts off as part-time. So now I'm juggling two part-time jobs, full-time school, religion, and family life. And you know what? I'm really enjoying it! That whole "It Gets Better" campaign was right. It actually does get better.

If I were you right now, I'd be expecting me to drop a bombshell right about here. But the thing is, I'm really trying to embrace imagining and seeing the good in a situation. It's not every day that you can just leave your entire old life behind you and go move across the country and meet new people and learn new things, so why would I bring with me the parts of me I've hated for so long? Easier said than done, but it's been good so far, and I'm running with it.

Soon enough, my video editing gig picks up, and I'm able to leave the restaurant biz behind me. Kitchen skills, gained. On to the next. At least I'm in the vein of what I'm going to school for, so my dollars aren't totally wasted.

It's a fun gig. Every once in a while, my boss throws me a bonus with my paycheck in the form of weed. See what I mean about this stuff just following me? How can I say no?

The guy I'm dating now has a brother who has fairly easy access to so many of the things I've tried to leave in the Midwest. I find myself faced with the opportunity to yet again dive into some psychedelics. Old habits die hard is an understatement. How can I say no? It's right here without me even trying.

So we pick a day off to do the thing. It started off good enough. The familiar slow creep followed by a sudden realization that I'm no longer in the same reality as much of the rest of the world.

I pick up a guitar and attempt to play a song I know. As I look down at the strings, I notice them producing a rainbow of colors as they vibrate. Confirmation that I've left the natural realm.

I attempt to continue to play for either moments or hours, I really can't be sure which one. As the vibrations from the strings continue, the color sends them out into the room, then inward, inside of me, and I become one with all things, yet nothing, all at the same time.

I can feel the vibration deep within my organs. Then I begin to feel my organs function individually like I never have before. I get visions of them rotting and melting inside me. I don't know if I'm feeling physical pain or if it's all in my head, but it's terrifying.

Turns out, this was my first bad trip. I spend the rest of the day trying to convince myself I don't need to go to a hospital. Then I spend the next several days wondering if any of my organs actually are rotting inside of me.

At the end of it all, I come to a very firm conclusion. Tripping is no longer fun. And I genuinely don't want to do that ever, ever again.

The opportunity actually came knocking on my door a couple times after that, and for the first time in my life, I turn it down. If you would have told me a couple years ago that I would ever reach a point where I'm turning down drugs of any sort, I would've asked for some of whatever you were clearly on. But here I am just turning it down all my own.

I wonder what I'm becoming.

I feel oddly vulnerable in leaving an entire genre of drugs behind me. It feels like I'm abandoning part of myself. My identity has been shaped by always saying yes to whatever kind of anything that crossed my path. I don't know who I am without these things, and now I have the audacity to be the one to rip myself away from it?

I feel lost. This is something I don't understand how to turn around and see the good in even though I've tried so hard to make that the theme of my new start. It doesn't make me feel good. In fact, I have to fight hard not to be sent into a depression over this.

This is probably part of new beginnings, right? They put you in a place of vulnerability to exploit the things in you that have to change. Because how else would you grow?

I just wasn't expecting this to hurt like it does. On top of that, it's not like I have anyone to talk to about this. I mean, who's going to empathize with someone deciding to no longer indulge in psychedelic drugs? The people I could talk to about it haven't made the same decision I have, and they don't understand it.

And it's not like I could bring that one up at church. "Hey, Mom and Dad, I'm twenty-five, and I finally decided to stop doing hallucinogens for fun!" I'm sure they'd be so proud.

There really is so much in life that is just out of my control. But deciding to consume various substances does not fall into that category. I guess for a long time, I believed the opposite of that. Like I had no choice, and I had to seek out and consume whatever I possibly could at all times because I had no other way of defining who I might be.

And now that I've made the choice to step out of that way of thinking and living, I have to have something to replace that void. So who am I? And how does anyone figure that out for themselves? The mild irony that the overwhelming feeling that question creates makes me want to do anything to avoid being sober long enough to figure that out is not lost on me. This circle is incredibly frustrating, which probably contributes to why I haven't broken free of it until now.

I start to try to look at church through a different lens. Growing up, people never really seemed happy to be there. Truly, I never understood why we had to go when everyone would clearly rather not be there. But at this new place, it's different. It's like the majority of these people seem content. Dare I even say…joyful?

It's like they know something, like they have something figured out that I'm trying to figure out. After a while of mandatory attendances, it even almost starts to feel like they have something I might want.

How do they maintain that level of contentment? I seriously doubt anyone else there drinks as much as I do, which is still my source of contentment. I'm probably the only one coming in hungover. Yet week after week after week, there's such consistency in everyone.

Even when they tell me about hard things they're going through. Even when they're facing cancer, surgeries, unemployment, there's such consistency in their attitudes and perspectives. So many of them seem almost unfazed at some of these mountains they're facing. How?

I'm going over this in my head one morning on my way to work, trying to identify any missing pieces that I may have overlooked in this puzzle I'm trying to fit together. I'm nonchalantly flipping through the radio at a stoplight, and something grabs my attention.

Have you ever had a moment in life where you feel like you're on some candid camera show? Like something either so perfect or so perfectly ridiculous is happening, and it feels like someone must have put in some major effort to follow you around and go through all the trouble to make it happen at that particular moment in time?

Well, this is one of those moments.

The strings caught my attention. Man, am I a sucker for some stringed instruments, so beautiful. And then this lyric comes in, and, truth be told, it feels in that moment like it was waiting there in time just for me.

"Because I don't have to be the old man inside of me / 'cause his day is long dead and gone. / I've got a new name, a new life, / I'm not the same, / and a hope that will carry me home."[8]

Woah. Somehow this feels like the way to the answer I'm trying to find. The chorus goes on talking about being set free. But that bridge—that's me. I feel like I've got a new life here. My old self is starting to die, by my own hand.

What is this hope he's talking about? What's this freedom he's claiming he's living in? How do you get carried home by it all? He's clearly happy he's not the same.

I'm a little surprised I'm feeling this, but I'm happy I'm not the same either. I'm happy that I gave up psychedelics. I'm happy that I'm turning a new leaf, actually getting sobriety in me.

It feels kinda good to say that, to think that. It feels good waking up not regretting what I did the day before or feeling so sick because of everything I consumed. It feels straight up good, and I'm really relating to this song, to this moment.

The song finishes, and I leave it on the station. It starts playing these little ten- to thirty-second clips of different people who have called into the station, and they're sharing these stories. It's surprisingly powerful and not something I was expecting to hear at 8:45 a.m. Some people are happy, some of them are so overcome with emotion that they're just publicly crying, some of the stories are about hardship. But they all have this common theme.

All these people are talking about how they took this "thirty-day challenge." I learn this radio station is called Klove, and this challenge is something they apparently do every year. All these people are sharing how listening to only Christian music for thirty consecutive days has changed their lives in some manner. All of them are saying it's been a change for the better.

I guess I didn't realize Christian radio stations were a thing? Or that there are actually a lot of people out there who choose to listen to it. In my mind, hymns from the eighteen hundreds and early nineteen hundreds were what defined this genre. Or college choirs on old cassettes that were daring enough to maybe have another instrument besides a lone piano. Snooze city, pass.

But apparently this is a thing that has been brought into the twenty-first century. Who knew? I let another song play as I wrap up my drive into work. It's kinda good. There's like real instruments in it, and the singer isn't bad. It's like real music. Real music that's good. And I think it makes me feel encouraged?

I'm intrigued by all of this and, for some reason, feel compelled to take this thirty-day challenge. Punk and ska will still be there for me in thirty-one days. What is there to lose? And my current boss and his wife are really into yelling at each other nice and awkwardly loud at the office. I could use some extra encouragement right now.

Actually, I could use a lot of encouragement. They're constantly fighting because the small business they run is going under. The small business I work for. Our lifelines. We can all see it, and it's been a long time coming.

It takes me a couple days to work up the courage to do this, but I take that thirty-day challenge into the office with me. I'm actually really nervous for the first few hours I let it play. I'm kind of anticipating someone telling me to turn it off or ask what's wrong with me. But nothing happens—at least not on the surface.

I'm only a few days into this, but I'm taking it really seriously. There will be no music that crosses my ears that isn't from this radio station. I truly want to see if this changes me at all or opens my eyes to anything I've been missing. I mean, what's the point of doing something if you're not *really* going to do it?

Day one of week two of the challenge starts. It's a Monday. I go in to work, and something feels off. More than usual. I'm barely into the work day when my boss comes in and tells me they've finally made the decision to close the business for good. This is it. This is the end.

What happens next is the thing that really got to me.

So when your boss comes in and tells you that you will be unemployed in the near future and there's nothing you can do to change that, that's something that would normally evoke a lot of heavy emotion in oneself. Followed by all sorts of other questions, many of which point back to the reality of "how am I going to pay for what I need to survive?" and the like. It's stressful.

But the weirdest thing is, in this moment, I'm not stressed. In fact, there's like the strangest, most unjust sense of calm over me. What should be dread and worry is just calm.

It shouldn't be like this. There should at least be a moment or ten of sheer panic and wonder, at least a sense of wanting to fight for this and desire to turn it around.

But all I have is peace.

This does not make any sense. But the whole day continues on like that. In fact, the whole rest of the week played out like that. Even when my bosses were around me experiencing their own moments of dread, regret, and sadness, none of it soaked into me. It was like I was immune. Sober and immune. It doesn't make sense, but I don't think I care. This feels like nothing I've ever experienced before, but I'm pretty sure I like it.

I hit the help wanted sites again in week three of my challenge. I may have peace, but I also still have common sense. I still need a job.

I'm barely through the first few pages of job listings, and a company name catches my eye. It's the last major client I made a television commercial for, so I click on it. Some medical secretary position, not exactly the best use of my college-educated dollars spent, but it's there and it's there now, and I already know these people because I've already worked with them.

This is probably a good time to mention that up to this point, I've actually already applied to over two hundred jobs in the past ten months. Working in an environment of constant tension and yelling is not worth the college-educated dollars, even if it is in my field. It wears on you, and I've actually wanted an out for a while now.

So I apply to this medical secretary job. All I say in the cover letter is that I made their last commercial and I'd love to meet up again to discuss how I can benefit their company. No lie—I get the job offer before the week ends. Oh, and it comes with a raise. Get that bread.

But why? I'm obviously not qualified. I applied to several *hundred* jobs before this one, many of which I actually *am* qualified for.

I wonder in the back of my mind if somehow, some way, this thirty-day challenge had anything to do with the peculiar way this all just played out.

I wonder if this will haunt me the same way the old ladies did before I moved out here. I guess I'll find out in time.

I finish out my challenge before my new job starts. It's hard to pinpoint right now, but I feel confident that something in me actually did change.

It's like that new perspective I gained when I moved out here of trying to see the good in a situation has somehow joined some kind of positivity force field around me. After years and years of struggling with depression, it's not even fair to say this. Is it even fair to think this? I'm the one who lived it, and I feel this way.

But it's like this had a stronger impact on deeply changing my depression than any medication, drug, or relationship ever has so far.

It's only been a month.

I don't really understand this right now. But I know how I feel. And somehow, I'm genuinely the happiest I've been in years.

Is this the beginning of it? Is this how it started for everyone else I've met that comes off as someone who is joyful? There's just no way a radio station could've been a missing piece.

But something in me is just so *different*.

BREAK OFF WHAT'S BREAKING YOU

Every single failure you go through is a step
towards a future you just can't see yet.
—Neil Pasricha

WHAT IF IT WAS POSSIBLE to rewrite the script on your trench? What if the narrative between you and the thing that is threatening to tear you to smithereens is in fact fully changeable?

I know some of you may feel entirely insulted at that insinuation. I don't take that lightly. I know you might be going through one of the hardest seasons of your life right now, through one of the deepest tragedies you never thought you'd be facing.

Yet here we are. You, facing this seemingly insurmountable giant. And me, suggesting coming out of this is entirely possible. There's something more we need to understand about trenches before we fully surrender ourselves to them.

In the major offensives of 1915, 1916 and 1917 many trench positions were only held for a few days at a time before the next advance moved them on into what had been no man's land or the enemy position. These trenches were scratch affairs, created as the advancing troops dug in, and were sometimes little more than 18 inches.[9]

We have the ability to flip the script. I'm not saying it won't take work and effort, and I'm not saying you won't bleed a little bit more. But your trench can be more than just a hole in the ground you use as a sanctuary to live another day. You fully have the ability to use that trench as a weapon against your enemy. You can absolutely start fighting from where you're at right now.

Dummy trenches were a particular arrangement used in a defense line. The idea was to dig another trench near your advanced front line and leave it empty. This would lure your opponent into blowing their weapons on an empty trench while you remained close by in prime position to take your shot when your enemy was left vulnerable and empty. It creates an opportunity to gain the upper hand.

Do you think in those moments of vulnerability when those soldiers were digging those dummy trenches, any of them were ever doubtful it was worth it? Do you think any of them ever faced moments where they just wanted to give up completely? Do you think they ever felt so alone that the weight of that feeling made it hard to take a next breath? Do you think they ever thought they'd make it out alive?

And isn't that so much a part of it all? Part of the most deeply rooted evil the enemy always seems to get in us is the idea that our next effort, our next step, our next breath isn't enough. That it's too small to matter in the grand scheme of the war we're stuck in, that it won't ever make a difference.

More than trench foot, more than the lice and rats, more than the elements, more than the gangrene, the diseases, the artillery fire, the lack of sleep, lack of food, more than any and all of the physicalities you could face in war, the most dangerous blow you can take is succumbing to the idea that the small actions and efforts don't matter. Believing that eighteen inches won't make a difference. That no-man's-land is useless dead ground. That the miles and miles and miles you've already dug was for nothing. That even though you've stopped making your camp in your trench, moving quickly through the trench lines won't help you win the war. You endured for nothing, you lost for nothing, you sacrificed and struggled and bled for nothing. See, the secret of surviving the trench isn't just about surviving the physical threats faced.

Your enemy's goal is to get inside your head to destroy you from the inside out. To convince you that your next step is no more impactful or important than your last. To plant the idea that not only do your actions not matter, but you don't matter, and that you're foolish and dumb for not only trying but even wanting to try.

It is too easy to get distracted by the noise and the explosions and sheer chaos of the war going on around us. These distractions tend to shift our focus on protecting our physical body and failing to keep a wall around our minds. And that's been part of the enemy's plan all along. He knows that as soon as your guard is down over your thoughts, that's when he can sneak in and plant the seeds that keep us stuck. After that happens, all he has to do is sit back and wait to watch you stay stuck, suffer, and die.

Don't buy into the lie! Those small actions and efforts—they matter.

In fact, they're your secret weapon to not only getting out of your trench but to winning your war.

*****

I can't recall another time I saw someone communicate their misery as clearly as I saw on the day I went for my medical secretary interview.

I walked up to the window, résumé in my freshly groomed hands, smile on my face, looking particularly hirable. I said hello and introduced myself to the only staff member present and stated my purpose for being there. The woman looked at me, said nothing, and walked away. Somewhat puzzled, I proceeded to take an open seat in the waiting area next to the window. I assume the woman is going to get another member of the staff or my interviewer, so I stay close by. A moment later there's an abrupt and startling slam. It's a clipboard hitting the counter. I hear an angry mumble that I'm thankful I could make out as a direction to "fill out this application."

I stand up and say "thank you," and again the woman says nothing, scowls at me, and walks away.

I assume this is the woman I'm here to replace. She clearly, clearly hates this job and every moment of being here.

Fun fact about me: I absolutely love going to interviews. I love getting dressed up, I love the professionalism on both ends, I love the challenge of figuring out how to incorporate the company mission into my answers, I love figuring out the way the interview guide they're reading off of is set up and adjusting my answers to stay one step ahead of them—I love it all. If there was a job that was just going on interviews all day long, I would crush that.

Since this is what's going through my mind, this massively angry woman doesn't faze me. I'm actually thankful for her that she's leaving something that makes her so painfully miserable.

I nail the interview and accept employment just a couple days later. My training schedule is a few weeks long and will be in another one of their offices with a very experienced, patient, kind, easy-to-get-along-with woman a good several decades older than me. She's amazing, and everyone I meet is kind and professional. She tells me this role generally takes about six months to feel comfortable in, but I'm on the right track and doing well so far. Who knew there was so much to learn in a secretary job?

I'm still listening to this radio station even though my thirty-day challenge is over. That change that started in me of being the least depressed I've been in years has snowballed, and I am doing great! I feel like I could conquer the world.

The last day of my training arrives, and my trainer goes with me to my home office, the same one my interview was at. I'm excited to meet the people I'll be working with on a regular basis from here on out. I wonder if any of them have heard of this radio station that I've come to be so keen on.

We arrive to the office, round the corner to what will be my new work home for at least the next few years, and suddenly I can feel the color and life start to drain from me. I can feel my jaw drop.

And it's too heavy for me to do anything besides let it happen. I'm just too shocked.

It's her. The same woman who practically threw a clipboard at my head the day I came in for my interview. I'm stunned into a speechless and motionless existence, standing there with a dropped jaw, unable to form words as the weight of my new reality hits me full force.

She's in the same emotional state as the day of my interview. Maybe worse. The scowl never leaves her face. I try to start conversations with her, but her preferred methods of communication are walking away, scowling and saying nothing, picking up the phone to whisper and complain to another coworker in another office, or straight up yelling at me.

And I'm the only one who works with her in our tiny reception area. Just me and the jackal.

So this is great.

I'm doing my best not to get discouraged. After over two hundred job applications, I know how difficult obtaining employment is right now if you want to work outside of the fast-food game. And literally everyone else in the entire company is great. I just never really work with them. But they exist, and I'm grasping for silver linings.

It's a strange season in my life because outside of the office, I've been really embracing new experiences and quieting the persistent introvert inside. Which basically means you kill part of yourself for the greater good. Small talk and meeting new people has never been my specialty. But hey, if I can get myself college educated, master my kitchen skills, juggle adult life, then surely I can get decent at small talk. Just rip the Band-Aid off and go for it.

For some reason, I've gotten it in my mind that I should find a spouse. And because I apparently have developed an all-or-nothing mentality out of the blue, I sign up on every online dating platform I can find, which is a lot. I also start looking very actively at events going on around the city, which I currently live about a forty-five-minute drive away from one way.

Everyone I know is either married already or seriously committed. I'd be lying if I said holidays weren't discouraging on average, constantly being the only one bringing just myself. Friend get-to-gethers feel the same. And nobody has the power to change your life except for you, right? So here we go.

It's become the summer of dating! At least my wretchedly awful coworker makes for a decent story to break the ice. In short, I spent about half the year going on a date, on average, three to five times per week. I've dated what feels like at least half the city of Pittsburgh. By the end of it, I would get texts from people and have to seriously ask myself who they were and try to remember if I had already gone out somewhere with them or was still in the process of setting that up.

Did I get better at small talk? Sure did. Did I also begin to lose a sense of my own identity through that wildly crazy and very expensive process of going out to meet someone new at a place that was also new quite literally almost every other day for about eight months? Sure did. Did I find my spouse in that process? Hahaha. No.

It's a lot of driving, about an hour and a half minimum per date. Part of me feels like if I don't put in more effort, I won't be worth the date to the other person. And I'm a bit too embarrassed to invite someone over to my parents' house to hang out in the basement with me.

Plus being a bit groggy going in to work in the mornings helps make it more bearable for a while, kind of helped to numb me to the never-ending life-draining environment. Even though I know these attacks can't possibly be personal, it's still hard to keep that fact present when they happen.

The common response to my "good morning," if there are actually any words that are formed, are responses like "what's so good about it!" or me just getting ripped into for a very minor mistake or failure to notice something, usually before I even have a chance to set my things down. If you're less alert for these constant attacks, it's just easier to let it slide off you.

But I've experienced a bully before, and this isn't high school anymore. So I try talking to her.

In fact, I try talking to everyone. Our manager, other coworkers, people in other offices who've worked with her in the past, even the company president (multiple times). What I learn is that I'm dealing with a person who believes things are solved by screaming— yes, screaming—at other people until they do what she wants. I don't understand why this is acceptable behavior. We're grown adults.

It's not uncommon for things to get "accidentally" thrown at my person, to get whipped in the back of the head with forms, for this tiny angry human to get within inches of me while yelling about a mistake I didn't even make. To say it's draining is quite an understatement. But I refuse to meet her at that level she refuses to leave. I will not stoop down and join her, no matter how outrageous the attack. And that's some of the most draining part of it all.

Toward the end of my summer of going on dates with about one hundred different people, I also starting doing this thing I heard someone talk about on that radio station. It's called "church shopping." I guess I didn't know you were allowed to do that? Maybe just because I was always stuck with what I had as far as religion was concerned. But this is a thing people do that's apparently normal? Also, at least for me, shopping is usually an enjoyable experience. So to couple an enjoyable thing with a thing that has typically been an additional source of pain and shame for me, well, it's weird.

But what part of my life isn't weird right now. So I'm going to embrace it. I don't know what exactly I'm even looking for. How do you judge one place over another, what makes one better? Will I know it when I find it? Who knows. All I know is I'm, reluctantly, still living under my parents' roof, and church is still a condition of that agreement. The loophole is it finally doesn't have to be *their* church. And twenty-six years of my father's preaching has exceeded my limit.

I could just say I'm going to other places and go to, oh I don't know, someplace like a park, a friend's house, even a bar. And had it not been for that radio station coupled with me trying to embrace the new sober lifestyle, that's probably exactly what I would've done.

For how much I have to deal with in the office on a daily basis, I really would like to have a little extra encouragement for my mind. Who knows, maybe I'll even get some tips here and there for how to deal with her. And my habit of checking people's left hands for rings is alive and thriving. Maybe I'll get lucky and meet some people or a special someone through the process. My mind is open.

I try to find some larger places that have a more diverse age group. My only experience with church involves the majority of the congregation being either married with little kids or retired, and nothing in between. I'm really curious to know if it's like that everywhere. I can't be the only single mid-twenties adult with mild interest in this whole idea.

And it turns out I'm not! There's a couple months where I try a new place every week. Every now and then I would find a place that had a speaker who was good enough to get me back more than once. But in almost all of them, there are some young people. Much like the music variety on that radio station, this shocks me.

And it turns out almost none of these places are dictated by a lone piano and hymn books. In fact, a lot of them sing some of these songs I've heard and have things like live drums and guitars. Kind of like an abbreviated concert experience. I used to think the lone piano approach was the standard across the country. Turns out I just got stuck in one of the few places left in the country that chooses to continue on like that. Who freaking knew.

A lot of these places are a lot less "condemny" than anything I've grown accustomed to. Like they traded in the fire and brimstone for, for lack of a better term, a hippie-esque approach of love and acceptance without coming off fake. It's just like they're highlighting all the good parts instead of staying focused on the bad parts. They still acknowledge the bad, but they don't set up camp there and send you off feeling worse than when you showed up.

It's like nothing I've ever experienced before.

The more I expanded my search, you know what I found? Even *more* people who seem to have this deeply rooted joyful attitude. Like this is some sort of a common thing in life. In fact, some of these places have *hundreds* of these people who just show up every week with this consistency. I was not expecting any of this.

Overall, it's kind of a cool experience. But let's be real for a minute here—I'm really still just doing all of this because I kind of have to. Still rocking that basement bedroom with the parents. Still obligated to oblige.

A lot of these places are filled with nice people, and I've met some cool folks, and some of the songs are really catchy. But nothing really sticks with me past Sunday. Monday morning still rolls around every week, and I still have to go back into my personal hell of a work environment.

By this point in the game, I have a lot more insight. The jackal has been moved to every office in the company over her tenure. The company president has confided in me, in so many words, that the main reason she's still here is because they can't find evidence to write her up or fire her past the word of every front office worker in the organization. Legalities. I make all sorts of suggestions along the lines of cameras and recording every line at all times on the office phones. You'll have all the evidence you'd need within the hour.

Apparently, my ability to control my demeanor in incredibly challenging situations might be working against me. I'm not sure if he believes it's as bad as I'm relaying. And all the patients love me. It's not uncommon for people to bring small treats or little gifts from their vacations back for me, even plenty of handwritten notes and cards. Take that, jackal.

I regularly acquire the sympathies via phone call or email on a weekly basis from others who have been stuck with her in the past and am continually commended for my ability to not engage. Which is kind and all, but man does that not help anything. I continually ask to transfer and am continually denied. I'm beginning to believe they're keeping me here because I'm literally the only one out of about forty who won't return fire with fire. Because I refuse to believe screaming is ever necessary in an office job. Or most jobs. Call me crazy.

Another average Monday rolls around. A new patient walks up to my window, and I'm going over her information to make sure it's all correct. She has an email address that catches my attention—it's @amplify.com. I immediately assume it's a production company, and within seconds, I'm transported to a working world that's not this one. I can do production, and I am about to schmooze with this person like I've never schmoozed before. If this is an out, I am taking it and taking it quick.

I ask about it, and she tells me it's a church. I'm immediately deflated. But I'm still "church shopping," so I ask her more about it anyways. It sounds like a couple other places I've been. Live band, a couple hundred people. I let it sink into the back of my mind and continue on with my day. There's another place I want to go back to because some people my age asked me to join them for lunch, and making friends as an adult is uniquely challenging.

The week finishes, and another average Sunday rolls around. I'm getting ready to go back to the place I went last week, and I'm looking up directions. I click on their website to make sure I'm going back to the right place only to realize service starts in five minutes. I'm too late to catch the start, and I hate being that person who walks in after everything's already rolling. People always turn around and look at you, and it makes me feel judged. Pass.

I remember that @amplify from last Monday, and I google them. They have two locations, and the one closest to me also starts in five minutes. There's one in the city that I can make at noon, but it's a forty-five-minute drive. And there's not even a hot date waiting for me at the end of that drive. I talk myself in and out of it several times over the next ten minutes, then finally decide to just flip a coin on it.

My favorite teacher in high school always used the flip-a-coin method in class. He was the only staff member in that torturous sentence that actually saw me. He helped me survive that place and never judged me. To this day, he's one of my heroes. And to this day, I still flip a coin on decisions that have ended up with equal pros and cons lists.

So it's heads, and I'm just going to suck it up and drive to this church in the city. I guess I can try to find something else to do down there to make it worth my time. At least it's a nice day out.

I get down there, and the place is really neat. It's some sort of old bar, and there's garage doors for walls, kinda cool. I can hear pre-service music playing as I walk up. Good music. Stuff they don't play on that radio station, but wow, it's actually really good. There's maybe a hundred people around, and almost everyone is around my age. The whole place is younger. It's dark and moody, and it's inviting because it feels like a place I'd actually enjoy hanging out in. At least it's worth the drive so far.

A few people say hi to me as I walk in and find a seat. You know before when I mentioned that a lot of these churchie folk have this kind of joyful attitude about them? Well, it's like that here too, but like, almost on crack. Like there is something really different happening here. And it's drawing me in.

The service starts with a little video they put on the screens. It's a smaller space in general, and two screens feels like overkill, but they're there. Then the band starts, and there's all these lights. I kind of feel like it's almost a bit…showy. Like they're trying too hard to put on an experience or something. Then it hits me that maybe I'm actually being judgmental.

The irony.

I laugh to myself and try my best to quiet my mind and just take it all in. Their pastor comes up on stage, and they do announcements, general church stuff, and continue on to the sermon. It's the first Sunday of the year, and they're starting a new series called Stronger. And I'm getting more sold by the minute.

He starts talking about ways to be stronger in your life and details challenges that I swear he pulled straight from my life personally. Like beyond candid camera kind of eerie, I swear he's talking straight to me. There are moments that it feels like it's just me and him in the room. Me and this total stranger. How could he have that much insight?

And it's not just insight. It's advice on top of insight. This is actually really helpful. This is actually something that's going to stick with me past today. This is actually encouraging and can actually make a real difference in my mind and in my life.

He finishes speaking in a dramatic crescendo as the band joins him, and they transition into this song.

I had no idea this moment was about to change my life completely.

The lyric "Mercy roars like hurricane winds / furious love laid waste to my sin"[10] hits the screens and hits my heart. The hundred voices around me fade into the instruments, and I close my eyes as the lyrics resonate in me. It's another moment in my life where time seems to be suspended and irrelevant. But this time it's not because of an impending OWI.

The lyric plays over and over in my mind. I'm flooded with hundreds of memories of my "sin," of all the bad choices I've made. Of *all* the drugs I've consumed. All the alcohol I've stolen and consumed. All the times I've put other people in danger because of my decisions.

All the times I've felt like the people I've gone to for help couldn't possibly care any less about me. The loneliness, the pain, the regret. The shame. It wasn't just the drugs that motivated the move to Pennsylvania. It was all of this. This whole entire life I wish I could somehow change or leave behind me. It's flooding me like a panic attack I can't control.

But the point of the song is…none of that matters.

It doesn't matter. And it doesn't matter because it's been forgiven. Because there's a love that is greater than I can comprehend, rushing in with a force like a hurricane, and that love cares about *me*.

I feel a rush come up from my toes that brings goose bumps followed by a wave of heat all throughout my body.

The song begins to come to an end, and I realize I'm sobbing. Not just like a little misty-eyed trickle—we're talking full-on sobbing, ugly crying in public.

I try to regain some composure as the next song begins, and I'm desperately hoping no kind soul tries to ask me if I'm okay. I have no idea what's happening right now. I haven't ever sobbed in public before. But I can't stop. Something in me just broke, something that needed to break.

I'm not sobbing because I'm sad. I'm crying because after all this, at the tail end of being twenty-six years old, after all the times I so firmly believed that there was nothing for me, no one to care about me, no one who saw me, thought about me, gave the slightest flip about me, after mulling over the decision to move states away from all I've known for months and months, after letting a church I hated back into my life only to be slowly lulled into church shopping, only to have this particular place dropped into my lap with the jackal five feet away from me, after all this. It's just not a coincidence.

The message, this song, this atmosphere, the fact that I'm *still* crying and no one's making it awkward or trying to interrupt. It's the fact that I don't feel judged, and I can just let this experience and this moment drench me. I know it with everything in me, with every ounce of all that I am.

This is finally *it*.

This is what I've been searching for this whole entire time.

It's not the building, although it's nice. It's not the pastor, although son can preach. It's not the music, although it's the best I've heard in my half year of venturing out to new places.

It's this encounter. It's this flood washing over me through every inch of my body. It's this feeling of peace, of acceptance, of hope, and of love.

I've heard people say things like "God meets you right where you are" before. I think back to the time when I was a teenager sitting in my room, crying because all I wanted to do was give up and give in. I think of how I prayed over something as silly as a dirty Kleenex to make it into a garbage can and how it immediately happened.

And I'm thinking about how my only goal was to find some church that I didn't hate and maybe make some friends. I prayed for a place that could just make me feel comfortable.

It's not just a coincidence that the words "Welcome Home" greeted me when I walked in to this place. It's not just a coincidence that this guy was basically speaking directly to me. It's not just a coincidence that this worship song has clearly totally wrecked me.

And this feeling in me.

It's no mistake this is happening right now. I was meant to be here, in this place, in this moment in time, for this exact encounter to happen to me.

I literally just had an encounter with God.

And I feel like that flood of hundreds of memories came rushing to the surface of my mind so they could be carried away, finally, by the only one strong enough to handle it all. He made it all flood up so he could carry it away from me.

He met me right where I was back as a teenager, and he's doing it again right now. Because this is specifically what I asked for. And I'm sobbing because for the first time in my entire life, I truly accept him. I feel whole in a way I have absolutely never felt before. There's just no substance or person that could ever match or duplicate this encounter, I'm certain. For the first time, I feel free.

For the first time, I feel loved.

Genuinely, on a level like I've never felt or never been open enough to feel before. On a level like I never imagined was possible. This moment is lasting a lifetime, and I want to live in it for another lifetime at least.

And it's all happening because of church.

Using My Down to Push Me Up, Not Out

Sometimes God allows us to feel the frailties of human love so that we can feel the real strength of His love.
—C. S. Lewis

W E CAN SPEND SO MUCH of our life in the trenches that we forget there's still more going on in the war around us. The warmth of the sun greeting our skin for the first time in years captivates the moment when we finally get out and relaxes our attitude to the larger picture at hand. We let our minds wander into the open fields of freedom, and we forget there are still unfound land mines waiting for us. Momentary relief makes it incredibly easy to forget to stay prepared for what we're about to face once we get out. Remember, your enemy has a tool kit too.

German ace Max Immelmann developed what became known as the Immelmann turn, in which an attacking fighter dove past the enemy craft, pulled sharply up into a vertical climb until it was above the target again, then turned hard to the side and down so that it could dive a second time.[11]

There's something powerful that happens when you learn to leverage your down. Your enemy already has this tool mastered, and with it, his goal is get you down and out. Yep, you personally. You have a target on you. We all do.

This fact isn't meant to be a discouragement. Rather, a weapon in your arsenal. Use it as a means to stay one step ahead as opposed to allowing yourself to become smothered under that truth over time.

I know it's easier and more comfortable to stay under that weighted blanket of discouragement in your trench. "Woe is me and my bright-red target. And my matching bright-red wound. It's not fair, it's hard, and I have a right to be upset about it and act however it makes me act." And that's exactly what he wants. But you're stronger than that, better than that, and you deserve so, so much more than that.

It can be daunting knowing we live under a state of constant attack. But doesn't that explain so much in life, really? I know you've had times in your life where it just feels like one thing after the next, after the next until it snowballs into an avalanche of a life you don't recognize as yours anymore. Maybe you're there right now?

The truth is, we can choose to remain discouraged, or we can choose to learn the patterns of the enemy and learn how to fight back.

I know, some of you are thinking, *That's easy for you to say, you have no idea what I'm going through. If it were as simple as trying to look at it a different way, don't you think we'd all be doing that instead of going through _____? Don't you think if I had any way of changing this situation, I would?*

That's exactly my point. Those thoughts and that kind discouragement are from the enemy, and we must learn to start recognizing the weapons he uses against us.

"But I didn't even cause this situation to be happening. It's being done to me. There's nothing I can do to change this." I hear you, and I have no doubt that's true for a lot of us.

Do you know what else is true? There's someone who has already claimed victory over the enemy you're facing right now. Someone who wants to be on your team, someone who is just waiting for you to ask them to fight for you and with you.

The biggest goal of your enemy is to keep you from finding this person and allowing them to fight on your behalf. To keep you isolated in your struggle.

You can be upset that you're already in the deep end, sure. But now it's your choice to listen to the enemy, give in and drown, or leverage the bottom to push yourself back up to the surface, back to the help waiting to carry you to victory over this thing.

What are you going to choose?

*****

I feel like I could dance through the streets as I leave this new place. I must be glowing. I want to sing! I want to hug strangers! I want to share this thing that just happened to me! This is better than ecstasy. It's like being in love, but better. It's literally brighter outside. It's the best thing I've ever experienced in my entire life. I want more!

I can't wait for next week. Honestly, if I can have this kind of hope and real joy on a regular basis, there's no Monday morning that can even faze me right now. Nothing is fazing me right now! I've finally found what I've been looking for my whole lifetime. There's nothing more I need or want.

But right now there is more! My golden birthday is coming up next month. I've just met someone who I believe to be my actual soulmate online, and we've been whisked into a whirlwind romance. And even though we live a state apart, we're making plans to meet for the first time.

My best friend in this world is coming out to visit me for my birthday next month, and we're even going to catch a concert while he's in town of one of both our favorite bands for years and years. He was my last roommate before I moved, and I haven't seen him in too long. I couldn't be more excited.

There's a lot going right.

There's also a really heavy thing going on in my family right now. Which feels almost surprising for this late in life. But my brother is fighting some demons of his own right now, and he's losing. He's been in and out of ICU at various times over the greater part of this year. I guess we've been on very different journeys through our twenties.

Pretty much our whole family is involved at some point or another. At times, it feels like overkill. Other times, I get glimpses of how close he really is to death itself. My folks can't hide how they're falling apart over this.

But right now we're in a good stretch, and things seem to be back under control, at least from what we can see. It's challenging not to live in a constant state of "what if?". There are so many dark places the mind can cling to so quickly if you're not careful. Maybe the hardest part of it all is feeling so helpless while looking imminent destruction and despair dead in the eye.

Probably one of the biggest misconceptions I believed for so long was an idea that if you found God, life isn't bad or hard anymore. It's supposed to be like a golden ticket to the cushy life, VIP access to easy street. Turns out, that's one of those whispers from the enemy he uses to get you to betray your help when life comes at you. Believing in God doesn't put you in some impermeable bubble here on earth. But it does give you a shield, a sword, and some other essentials you'll need in the fights.

So in the lull between frontline warfare, I have a couple of really good things happen and get in place for me to look forward to. And I'm taking them while I've got them.

I pick up my best friend from the airport a couple of days before my birthday. I try more than a few times to get him through the front doors of my new church just for one service, just for a little over an hour of life. I know if he could just get even the slightest taste of what I did, his life would change completely too. I love him too much not to try. Everything in me wants this for him. How could you not want this for someone you love?

Or even for people you don't love. Maybe they would suck a lot less if they knew how much could be different for them.

He turns me down every time I ask about the Sunday coming up, so I don't push him. I just continue to share how much in me has changed since all this came into my life. Maybe that's enough. It's still amazing just to see him again and spend time together.

The day of our concert comes, and I am so excited. But he's not. He's really not feeling too well, and he looks it. We debate skipping it, but it's really not every day you get to see a longtime favorite in another state, especially with someone who makes it mean that much more.

We go and we hit the balcony of the venue since there are seats up there. It's a great show, but I can tell he's not himself at all. His flight out is the next day. I hug him against his will at the airport and tell him I love him. I really hope he feels better soon.

Just a couple days after that, my new romance and I meet up for the very first time. There's a trip planned from the other side of Ohio clear to Hershey, Pennsylvania, with a stop in the middle to meet me over the weekend. A plan not from my creation but one that I'm pretty happy about.

Something's not right when we meet in person though. You know sometimes how you get that feeling in you that something's just off? Like that little voice inside of you or whatever that nudges a red flag into your field of view. It's disappointingly that. That plus something else I just can't put my finger on. Something deep in me feels really off.

The trip to Hershey is happening on Monday. All weekend I debate calling in sick to work to make the six-hour round trip venture to some chocolate museum. Naturally, I flip a coin on it. It's heads, so for the first time in this job, I call in and spin a tale of some sushi that really had it out for me. Food poisoning. I feel guilty for a minute, then I'm just thankful it's one less day of the jackal in my life. The guilt melts quickly.

It's a beautiful day for a road trip though. Early March, spring is trying to spring, the sun is out, the weather is fantastic, and the thrill of lying to get out of responsibility for the first time since high school is giving me an all-day rush.

We get to the museum before noon. We're about halfway through, and I'm reading some educational-about-junk-food plaque, and I get a text from my mom.

She's asking me if I'm at work. What the heck is going on, and why am I nervous all of a sudden? I answer back that, at the moment, I'm not in the office. It's around lunchtime, so I feel that's all the detail I need to provide. Did my boss call my parents or something? What is this?

She asks if I have time to talk for a minute, so I call her. She asks me again if I'm in the office, and I just say not at the moment. Something's really off, her voice is heavy. I ask what's going on. She asks me if I'm alone, and I can tell something bad happened. I cut through the crap and demand to know what's going on.

My sister-in-law saw a post on Facebook. Everyone knows I don't participate in the socials, so she's calling to tell me something.

Tyler died. My best friend in this world. I just saw him five days ago. I just hugged him. This can't be true. I tell her she's lying, it's just not possible. I can't comprehend this.

It feels like a scene from a movie. All I can hear is high-pitched silence. There's a ringing in my ears, and I feel like I'm going to pass out. I crumble to the floor in the middle of this stupid museum in the middle of the worst Monday of my life just trying to breathe. I have to get outside. I can't tell what reality is anymore, and I just have to get outside.

I can't even cry. I can't even speak. I can't tell if this is true. The weight of this all is crippling, yet I feel too numb to exist.

The next morning, I hear my dad talking on the house phone. Tyler's mom found their number and is desperate for any details on his last days. She lets us know his funeral will be Saturday in the town we grew up in. It'll be about twenty-four hours' worth of driving in about two and a half days. I'd walk there if I had to. This is the last thing I'll ever be able to do for him. I know no one else on this planet will be able to give him the eulogy he deserves.

How does anyone get through things like this?

I go into work to ask for bereavement time. I'm told it only applies to family, my response to which is he is my family. I try not to let myself become bitter at the denial of time out of the office. It's hard to fight that. I get my Friday covered, so I can at least have a little extra time for the 1,200-mile round trip. It takes everything in me not to cry constantly throughout the day. It's impossible actually, and I take several extended breaks in the bathroom throughout the week. At least the jackal is leaving me alone right now.

I spend my time in between work trying to write something I can say on Saturday. I spend even more time just crying. And, let's be honest, rum makes quite an appearance in my life again.

I don't know how to get through something like this.

Yet with everything in me, I know there's more. With everything in me, I want to believe I'll see him again one day. Even though he never got to have an encounter like I did, maybe our conversations around it was enough. Even death bed confessions and acceptions arrive in plenty of time to change your eternity. Right now that's the only hope I have left to cling on to. So I cling with everything I've got.

My mom graciously offers to make the drive with me and even gets us a hotel room. Support systems mean the world through tragedies.

The feeling of driving back into the hometown that nearly killed me multiple times over fills my stomach with lead. We get there the night before his funeral, and I go out with some other friends I haven't seen in years. War buddies. Somehow we're the ones left who've survived this place. At least the weight of grief overpowers all of the sickness just being here brings.

I'm surprised to see well over one hundred people show up for his service when I get there. It's kind of like a high school reunion. My first roommate even shows up. We haven't spoken since we moved out. I'm shocked. I'm also wildly hungover and running on about three hours sleep. From all I can tell, the hotel we were in rented the rest of our floor to a very nocturnal family of wild elephants who apparently just did straight shots of espresso all night and were afraid of going outside to burn off their energy, so they used the hallway. Quite unfortunate.

I go inside the funeral home as it starts to fill up. Did any of these people even know him? Majority are faces I don't recognize. I find his parents and ask them if it's all right if I read something on his behalf, and they welcome it.

Mere moments later, of all people, the pastor who took over my dad's church after we all left steps up to the podium and announces me. I'm briefly shocked that I'm opening the service and immediately thankful I already wrote everything I wanted to say down so I could just read it.

I walk up to the front and take off my glasses so I can't see the crowd. Public speaking was absolutely never my strong suit. Mix that with extreme grief and you get, well, someone crying and shaking at the podium, trying to put on the facade to the staff that I'm not going to pass out or collapse on the podium itself. I let the room know there's no way I'll be able to get through this without crying and begin to read.

"Hi, I'm Bekah. Tyler was one of my best friends for over a decade.

"Most people on their initial reaction to Tyler would probably think he's just this tall, quiet, shy guy who really loves metal and crappy '80s music. He was a man of few words and subtle expressions.

"We've been through more than a fair share of some hell and high waters together. Got in some trouble together, got out of some trouble together. We never fought, never argued. We could do anything together and still have a good time. I got to live with him in Milwaukee, and, though it had its challenges, it was always worth it."

You could a hear a pin drop on the carpet of this place. The silence is so thick as I spill out my heart to these strangers. I notice I'm still physically shaking, and I wonder if the silence is out of respect or suspense of what my body is going to do next. They don't know, and I'm right there with them.

"We could and did tell each other everything. Our thoughts, our fears, our dreams. We had made the plan to just get married." There's a collective group "awe," and I laugh at them and say he would have laughed at that too. I restart the sentence and am able to finish the ending of it this time. "We made a plan to get married to each other if we were both still single with no prospects after we both hit thirty.

"Years ago we were wandering the streets of this town late one night, just talking, and in the depths of the conversation, he told me if the choice ever had to be made, he would die for me. And I told him with certainty I would do the same.

"I've spent the past week trying to think of a particular story that I thought was funny, or a moment that was particularly memorable, a little glimpse that perfectly captures the epitome of our friendship, our bond, and our time spent together. Something that I could share to emphasize what a truly sweet and loving person he was and how much he means and will always mean to me.

"There are so many examples of happiness and good times that come to mind. Tyler is and always will be so much more than what a few words at his funeral would be able to describe. He's part of me.

"And now having that part of me gone has flooded me with some of the heaviest despair I have ever felt in my life. Tyler was always there for me and I for him. We got each other through so much. And now to know he's gone tears through my core in a way I never thought possible.

"I feel very shattered. I know without a doubt I do not possess the strength it's going to take to get through this loss."

I pause. Partly to clear my eyes so I can see the next paragraph, partly to let the moment build, and partly because I'm saying this next part more for me than for anyone else. This is the most important part of all of it, and I need the truth to be clear and loud, said with confidence. I take a deep breath, and I can feel some fragility shake off of me. It feels like someone else's strength is guiding my words. Somehow the tremble leaves my voice as I continue.

"But in the depths of this great despair, I find my peace in this promise. Isaiah 43:1 says, 'Fear not, for I have redeemed you: I have called you by name; you are mine. When you pass through the waters, I will be with you; and when you pass through the rivers, they will not sweep over you. When you walk through the fire, you will not be burned; the flames will not set you ablaze. Since you are precious and honored in my sight, and because I love you.'

"We have promises of protection, of guidance. We have a lighthouse to get us through the storm and an anchor waiting for us to keep us safe.

"I don't have the strength to get through this. But God has promised he does, and that I can find my strength in him. John 16:33 says, 'I have told you these things, so that in me you may have peace. In this world you will have trouble. But take heart! I have overcome the world.'

"When I think about how overcome with despair I am in this, I counter it with these questions from something I read recently:

"'Can betrayal take your joy? No, because Jesus will never leave you.

"'Can failure take your joy? No, because Jesus is greater than your sin.

"'Can sickness take your joy? No, because God has promised—whether on this side of the grave or the other—to heal you.

"'Can death take your joy? No, because Jesus is greater than death.

"'Can disappointment take your joy? No, because though your plan may not work out, you know God's plan will.

"'Death, failure, betrayal, sickness, disappointment. They cannot take your joy, because they cannot take Jesus from you,'[12] and he promised us again in John 16, 'Now is your time of grief, but I will see you again and you will rejoice, and no one will take away your joy.'

"Yes, this is a heartbreakingly sad day and season of life now. And this is going to hurt for a long time, probably the rest of my life. But there is a strength and a hope in me that will carry me through this valley of weeping. There is a love that is going to make me stronger as it carries me, a hope that is never ending and never failing, and a love that will never let go of me.

"This is going to be us one day. Each and every one of us. And no matter when that particular day is for you, it is always going to feel like it's too soon.

"Simply because I didn't know the particular depths of his heart before he left, I can't, with any sort of certainty, say where I think Tyler is now.

"But what I can say with certainty is that those of us left here have a very real hope and a very real promise, and all you have to do is believe in it.

"'No eye has seen, no ear has heard, no mind has conceived what God has prepared for those who love him.'[13]

"Tyler, I hope I see you there."

I return to my seat and unashamedly let out a sob that fills the room as my friend pulls me into his shoulder. How does anyone get through something like this? With help. By relying on strength that's not our own. By pressing into the only one who promised to never leave us and never forsake us. By abandoning the idea that we're strong enough by ourselves—we're not. By believing all of those promises from God are actually true and, on top of that, that they apply to you personally. Because they do.

I don't for a second believe this kind of grief ever leaves a person. Time doesn't really heal those kinds of wounds. But what does happen is we grow. We get stronger as time goes on, and the weight of tragedy becomes more bearable because the strength within us multiplies.

These are the kinds of forks in the road where we have to decide. Am I going to go back into my trench under this new weight of despair? Because I know my trench well. The comfort of it sure would feel nice right now. It sure would be easier just to return to doing whatever I could to momentarily escape feeling these terrible feelings right now. The familiarity sure would feel nice in the midst of everything this new reality is bringing into my life that I hate. Wouldn't it just be so much easier to slip back down to what you already know?

These are the kinds of forks the enemy loves to use in your life. He waits for these and rejoices when we get hit because his goal is always to get us back into the trench. His goal is to make us believe our feelings are more true than the promises given to us. And when tragedies strike, because they will, because we live on a broken earth, he loves to help us believe that we'll never recover from the blow, and he loves to help guide us back into the trenches we know so well.

So many of us openly believe his lies while actively pushing away help. We believe things like "God's not on your side. If he was, why did your best friend just die at twenty-eight?" And we're quick to believe the lie because the enemy gets up in your face, right up in your business.

God doesn't force his way into your life, because if he did, we'd all be mindless God-loving robots; it'd be meaningless. He doesn't force his way in because he loves us enough to give us the ability to choose for ourselves. But the enemy doesn't operate on the same playing field. He comes right in whether you accept it or not. He's there fully loaded.

And he's gotten really good at making us believe that when tragedies happen, we don't have another choice other than returning to our trench. That's not true!

Unfortunately, most of us only learn how to leverage our down by actually being down. It's not a skill you learn remotely, you learn by going through it. It's the tragedies that teach us how to look up because they leave us with almost no other option.

But a lot of us stay down because we choose to believe the lies the enemy throws at us while we're there. That this will never get better, it will never change, it will never get easier, we'll never get stronger, never recover. Sound familiar?

This is where choice comes in. Can you choose to magically change the situation you're in? Can you choose to poof away the disease or the loss? Of course not. But that doesn't mean you're out of options. All that means is the options that seem easiest to us aren't accessible. It just means the options that are going to help us and actually get us through just take a little more work than the ones we'd prefer. We must learn to identify the lies and to stop accepting them as the truth.

One more important thing to know in this phase of the battle—after you level up your game and start to get good at discerning the lies, the enemy will level up his game too. His goal will never be anything other than trying to take you out, and he's got a lot of energy. Remember, this knowledge is part of your path to victory, not a doom-and-gloom cloud that only hangs over you.

If you feel like you don't have the strength to try one more time, then surrender. Not to the trench, but to your helper. Your down can be a place for you to catch your breath. To recover. Restrategize. Fix your lens. Adjust your armor. This isn't the end. Let this be the beginning of your surrender to the right thing. It's not too late. You are not too far gone. You are not unfixable or unhelpable. You're no lost cause.

You might just be down here right now because that's where you need to be for the right roots to start taking hold and start growing. Use the darkness of the depths to your advantage. Start planting the seeds while the enemy can't see you down there so after they start growing, they add to the force that pushes you up out of this thing.

Trees don't grow from sapling to full height overnight, and neither will you. It might just feel dark for a little while. That's okay. It's not something we need to fear, dread, or resent. It's just a necessary part of the process.

So what does the whole process look like? And how do we know we're going through it correctly?

Baby Steps Are in Fact Still Steps

*Shame grows in the dark and can become a major burden if left
unchecked. But it loses a lot of its power in the light! The more you
connect with others and relate, the less alone and helpless you will
feel. The more you open up, the more perspective you gain from
others, the more support you have the less power shame has.*
—Melissa Urban

E VEN THOUGH WORLD WAR I has long ended, there are still millions of us living in the trenches right now. Here's some sobering truth.

Suicide is the tenth leading cause of death in the United States.[14]

More than eight hundred thousand people die by suicide each year globally, which is one person every forty seconds.[15]

Suicide is the second leading cause of death among individuals ages ten to thirty-four. There are two and half times as many suicides as homicides.[16]

Forty-two percent of LGBTQ youth seriously considered attempting suicide in the past year. Thirty-one percent of native or indigenous youth attempted suicide, twenty-one percent of Black youth, twenty-one percent of multiracial youth, eighteen percent of

Latinx youth, twelve percent of White youth, and twelve percent of Asian/Pacific Islander youth.[17]

Middle-aged people, especially men, have the highest rate of suicide compared to other groups. Eighty percent of all deaths by suicide in the US are among men and women age forty-five to fifty-four. Men ages eighty-five and older have the highest rate of any group in the country. Many factors contribute to this risk, including isolation, a history of violence, and access to lethal means.[18]

The overall suicide rate in the US has increased by thirty-five percent since 1999.[19]

Why am I bombarding you with this information? Because suicide and mental health in general is still some of the most stigmatized issues we face in the US and around the world. We feel like we shouldn't talk about our struggles, like we can't give face to the trials. We feel like we're broken and we should hide that fact. We feel ashamed.

These statistics don't happen overnight. People don't just snap all of a sudden and end up adding to these numbers. It's all the little things in life that get to us. Over time, they add to the weight we carry around. It's the slow build that helps us arrive at these kinds of destinations.

We also recently saw the largest increase in the last fifty years of drug overdose deaths. A stunning ninety-three thousand in the US, up thirty percent from the year prior.[20] Worldwide, that number is closer to half a million people.[21]

Data from private health care claim records show that self-harm also spiked dramatically recently, seeing an increase of 99.8 percent.[22]

It's arguable that were 5 to 10 major battles that happened in World War I before it finally came to an end. But the overall number of battles in those four years is closer to a total of 225.[23]

That's four very long years where people all over the world had absolutely no idea how, when, or if the war was ever going to end. They had no idea if what they had to offer was anything close to enough to make any sort of difference in it all, no clue if the next battle was the last or if there were still one hundred more waiting after that. Yet despite that discouragement, day after day, month after month, millions of people chose to fight on.

That war wasn't won overnight, yours won't be either. That war wasn't won after the first battle was fought. Or the second or the third or the fourth. Yours likely won't be either. The war wasn't won after the first injury was received, after the first bout of discouragement was experienced, after the first loss was walked through. Yours won't be either.

But what did happen after years of determination, after years of investing in learning the patterns of the enemy, years of getting stronger after walking through the valleys, going through the losses and continuing to press on, eventually, the war was won. It was won because millions of people continually decided to take *one* step in the right direction.

This is why the small efforts matter.

It's time to stop believing the lie that baby steps are worthless. Baby steps kill us when we start taking them in the wrong direction. The numbers don't lie. They also clearly don't discriminate. This applies to us all.

It's easy to see the trial in your life and default to a mentality that says you deserve the trial because you've done something. That's just another enemy tactic.

No one fights for things that don't matter. The struggle, the trench, the trial in your life right now is evidence of your worth, not lack of worth. There's a war going on around you because *you* are worth the fight. There is love going after you, and there is the enemy going after you. Because you are a beautiful prize, a treasure to be had. You are valuable.

For a lot of us, it's easier to admit there's an enemy than a God, because we can more easily see what the enemy is doing in our lives. Cue in the disease, the breakup, the unemployment, the loss, the car problems—you name it. Remember, the enemy will get right up in your face whether you choose to believe he's real or not. God waits for you to make the first move.

You already know the enemy's real. So why are you still fighting to reject your helper? It's time to stop believing the lie that no one's for you. That's a tactic that doesn't deserve to have victory over you anymore.

The next battle you're about to face isn't a sign that you're losing the war. It's a sign that you're on the right path. It's a sign that you're building forward momentum. It's a sign that you're one step closer to triumph.

Shaking off the shame will take practice. It likely won't come easily right away, but nothing really does when we're first learning it. That's okay. If you're in the dark at the bottom of your trench, know that the first few steps you start taking are going to take a little bit of courage, because you won't be able to see a glimpse of light until after you've already started moving.

Just keep moving.

*****

Somehow an entire year and a half has passed. It feels like so much has happened, yet at the same time it feels like I just finished the drive back home from the funeral yesterday. There's not a day that goes by that I don't think about him.

A few months after I got home, I saw an article online that a band we both loved was releasing a new record soon. In my excitement, I'd literally picked up my phone to text him. I actually got to the letter T before reality, in a cruelly, somehow shockingly freshly painful way, reminded me of my now forever present void. Another reminder that time and the rest of the world moves forward whether we choose to stay stuck or relive moments, wishing for different outcomes. I wonder how much longer until all these small moments in life will stop echoing pain.

I have to fight feeling guilty sometimes when moments of happiness happen. It's strange how mourning can sneak in and warp your view of certain emotions. As if anything would be able to bring him back or make me suddenly wake up from a coma only to learn it was all a dream.

The jackal is really wearing on me. The majority of the days on my drive into work now I cry. It feels so much like a prison sentence.

Year three with no end in sight. How does someone stay so, so angry for so long, so unrelentingly? I don't understand, and I'm back to making applying for new jobs my other full-time job.

I don't know how I'd be making it through without Amplify. I know if it wasn't for that, I'd just be getting back in to drugs on a full-time basis again. I may have dabbled a bit here and there in the past year. Turns out, it'll just never stop coming into your life for free if you choose to continue to meet new people in the world.

I know I need to pull back in on this before I start actively seeking it out again. Gaining a connection and a supplier isn't something my body would be able to handle; my blood pressure's already through the roof at a resting rate. It's trying to warn me. And this time I'm actually listening.

There are these things called small groups at church. It's just groups of people who get together once a week to learn about a given topic and hang out to discuss it and build relationships. I'd really like to meet some people who won't slip me something to snort next time I use the restroom. I just want to have some normal, healthy relationships. For once. I never thought I'd actually have to work this hard to get that in my life.

Apparently, even if you develop a relationship with God, followed by other healthy relationships with people, there remains that old part of you that still really enjoys the things you used to. Things like getting and being high. I guess I kind of thought that would all just fall off after I chose to let God in. It very much did not. It's something I have to actively deny. A lot of times it's very challenging to turn it down. I mean, I've spent half my lifetime hardwiring my body and mind to love it.

The more involved I get with things at church, the more surprised I am how deeply rooted the lie in me was that life gets easier when you start building a relationship with God. I don't know why I thought I'd suddenly become impervious to hardship or temptations the closer I got to him. Now there's this conviction when the temptations come. Sometimes it's hard to decipher that from guilt.

I guess this might be why some people give religion a try for a few months and then give up on it completely. Like it's a magic wand to a perfect life, and when you don't see the result you want quick enough or instantly, you call it a sham and walk away. Or we start to change the direction we're headed, but we mistake correction in our lives as punishment and take on guilt and shame because that's the only language we know to communicate with. So all we feel we can do is give up and call ourselves a failure again. We succumb to the attacks. They can be so subtle.

Anyways, I'd like to think it's not all hard right now. I've been in a relationship that I really believe is going to be my last one for life. Marriage is definitely on the table, and it really helps to feel like there's someone on your side through the fires. We're moving in together on our one-year anniversary. It feels like a redeeming factor for this current season of awfulness, so I'm ignoring the whispers in me that're trying to edge the red flags I kicked away back into my field of view. I feel like I need this, so it's happening.

But I'm still turning to alcohol for strength. I reason with myself that whenever I don't have to face the jackal the majority of my days is when I'll kick the spirits. I mean, look at how much I've already gotten rid of. Surely everyone deserves one vice.

That reasoning wears on me. Probably because it's riddled with holes. My brother is back in the ICU again. It's more life-threatening with every visit. Alcoholism sure runs deep in my family. I know I need to kick this last daily vice, even if it is my only one left.

I go to visit him on my day off work. I hate hospitals, and I'm generally not great finding things to say in situations that already look bleak with the odds stacked against you. It's hard to imagine any sort of positive spin I can add to any aspect of this whole situation. I don't want to imagine what's going to happen to our family if he doesn't see thirty-four.

It's kind of weird driving there by myself. I guess I thought if you had a spouse, they would go with you to support you in the heavy moments of life. Or at least offer or acknowledge how painful and hard the whole thing is. And where was my whole family when I was the one who needed help when I was just a kid? To this day, I have no idea if my dad knows, or even cares, that my mom took me to the ER as a teenager desperately trying to get help. Now he's involved with my brother, and so are his sisters and their husbands. The whole family. Why is my life so meaningless to the people who are supposed to at least pretend to care about me? Why didn't I matter enough to fight for?

I let my mind wander in the silence of the car in between my phone giving me directions. I feel stuck in such a fog. Will I ever feel normal again? When will it stop feeling like life is attacking me from every angle? It's too often that every waking moment just feels like a struggle again. It's been years since I thought about how meaningless my existence may be to the rest of my bloodline.

Suddenly, it hits me. I've been here before.

Yes, literally in the sense that I'm getting yelled at two minutes into my Monday morning shift. Again. Yes in the sense that as a family, we're all mentally trying to potentially prepare for a massively devastating loss. Yes in the sense that I stumbled and let a dose, or several, of hard drugs come back into my life for a night here or there in the name of fun. Yes in the sense that feeling completely meaningless to everyone "close" to me has moved into the forefront of my thoughts. It all really hollows you out pretty quickly.

This feeling of hopelessness… I have lived here before. I have embraced it before. I have let it rule my mind, my actions, and my life before. I've rolled over and let it kick me over and over while I've been down before. I've almost died from this before.

What I've learned since then is the fact that I have a choice on whether or not I build camp here again.

With everything in me, I am not going back.

I really wish making that decision made everything easier. I'd actually settle for anything, any aspect to just get a little bit lighter.

If my brother would even just sit up in the hospital bed and say a sentence to me. If my partner would just send me one encouraging text in lieu of absence. If a single one of these two hundred plus companies I've applied to would send me an email. If my check engine light would just stay off or this machine would stop costing me an extra $400 every other month in repairs to ease the stress of living paycheck to paycheck while I watch more debt pile up. If I could just muster up an ounce of meaning to justify my existence.

Anything. I would settle for any scrap of relief. But nothing comes.

I leave the hospital without my brother saying a word because he's mostly unconscious. My phone has no new messages or missed calls. The check engine light is still on, and there's not one single employment prospect on the line to release me from my unrelenting daily torture. Did this visit even matter? Does a single other person even care at all that I made effort? Do I even matter?

All I have is church in the morning.

On the drive back home, I decide it's time to fight. If I wait longer sitting idle in this swamp of poison, this'll take me out or force me back into my trenches. I recognize this pattern, this enemy. So I choose to focus on what I can control. I choose to meditate on the truth a loving fellow soldier left for me to find, a weapon to use in battles like these.

> I am passionately in love with God because he listens to me. He hears my prayers and answers them. As long as I live, I'll keep praying to him, for he stoops down to listen to my heart's cry. Death once stared me in the face, and I was close to slipping into its dark shadows. I was terrified and overcome with sorrow. I cried out to the Lord, 'God, come and save me!'

There's no reason to sugarcoat the pain or try to hide the fact that sometimes, we start slipping into places that utterly terrify us. There's no reason not to cry out for help, and there will be times in all our lives when that is the only option available to us. Sometimes our prayer, our communication and expression of our current state, is sorrowful, desperate. There is *no* shame in this. Look what happens when we're honest about that.

> He was so kind, so gracious to me. Because of his passion toward me, he made everything right and he restored me. So I've learned from my

experience that God protects the vulnerable. For I was broken and brought low, but he answered me and came to my rescue!

Now I can say to myself and to all, 'Relax and rest, be confident and serene, for the Lord rewards fully those who simply trust in him.' God has rescued my soul from death's fear and dried my eyes of many tears. He's kept my feet firmly on his path and strengthened me so that I may please him and walk before Yahweh in his fields of life.

Even when it seems I'm surrounded by many liars and my own fears, and though I'm hurting in my suffering and trauma, I still stay faithful to God and speak words of faith. So now, what can I ever give back to God to repay him for the blessings he's poured out on me? I will lift up his cup of salvation and praise him extravagantly for all that he's done for me. You have broken open my life and freed me from my chains. I'll worship you passionately and bring to you my sacrifice of praise, drenched with thanksgiving![24]

All I have is church in the morning. And right now there's nothing that could even come close to being everything I need more than that fact.

There's no end in sight for any of the mountains in front of me right now. But I have seen what he's brought me through before, over and over, and I have felt him right there with me in the past when I didn't even have the words or depth to put his name to the presence. I know confidently that he will not leave me. He never has. He won't fail to restore me after these trials are over, and he won't stop protecting me from one of the biggest aggressors from the enemy line—my own thoughts.

It doesn't make any of this any less painful. I still have to feel the hurt, the sadness, the confusion. I still have to walk through it.

But now it's with a new lens. A lens that says, "I don't know how or when you're going to get me through any of this. Even though I can't see how, I trust that you will. Because you have before. Because you promised you would. And I didn't even ask for help before, but you still came through for *me*. Because you listen to me and care deeply about the details of my life."

This is how a sacrifice of praise can turn into your weapon. I can't control the outcome of so many of the trials even though I want to and try to. It's a sacrifice to do what I can and then surrender my heart to trust him with the rest and release the outcome.

Even though it hurts, I am going to go to church tomorrow and sing at the top of my lungs, through tears, and confidently proclaim the goodness of God and his promises over my life. The other option is going back to the trench.

Both options will hurt in some manner.

But only one option has hope at the end instead of despair. Life instead of death. Mercy and goodness waiting around the next corner instead of destruction. I have to take the next step no matter which option I choose. I choose my next step to be toward him.

So I go to church in the morning and do just that. You know what changed about any of my trials after the service was over? Nothing. Not one single thing.

Right here is where the enemy gets a lot of us. Lies like "See? If God was so good, why didn't he change this for you after you sacrificed? Why's he still making you walk through pain? He doesn't really listen. He doesn't really care." The enemy creates forks in our roads in attempts to redirect us back to the trenches with these lies every single time there's an opportunity for it. Believing them is taking one next step in the wrong direction.

It takes some practice to learn the enemy's voice from our own. Our inner monologues, our recurring thoughts about ourselves, how we view ourselves and our reality—a lot of these foundations have the enemy's fingerprints all over them. They can be some of the hardest things to change because they've become so deeply ingrained over the course of our lifetimes.

We won't get out unless we first acknowledge where we are. What lies are you believing right now? We have to learn how to call it what it is, to identify the lies and mentalities masquerading as our comfort zones. Denying it just reinforces the trench walls and keeps us stuck.

Just because familiar thoughts and feelings of worthlessness are representing themselves in my life again does not make them any more true than the last time they made an appearance. All that means is the enemy has successfully identified a weak spot in me and is continuing to try to exploit that while I'm progressing.

These are part of the tactics. Our deepest wounds and hurts are the enemy's delights. Don't believe for a second that because you're walking through familiar pain that you deserve it or it's justified. You don't deserve it, but you do have to be able to identify it. If you don't, the option at the end of your road is returning to your trench.

Don't let the enemy win. The devil is in the details, yes. But so is your helper. It is your choice which one you look to. These small, seemingly meaningless decisions of what we let into our minds and what we choose to dwell on, these are the weapons. We can learn how to use them, or we can succumb to the damage as they're used against us. It's not "just one thought." That one thought can and will snowball if you choose not to take it captive, to name it as the lie that it is.

My life is not meaningless, it is not void of value simply because I've been overlooked by other imperfect human beings. They do not define me, validate, or invalidate my worth. The fact that I was questioning my worth was just evidence that I'm being fought for, evidence of someone else trying to take me out and steal my life before I could find my way back to the truth.

How many times do we repeat a different version of the same battle simply because we neglect to take the time to identify the patterns? It's so easy to get caught up in a way of thinking that tells us if people treat us a certain way, then we should expect the same thing from God. If religion treats me like this, why would God be different? If the people closest to me in my life could do things like this to me, and they're the ones who are supposed to love me, then how could love from any other source actually be anything good, anything worth fighting for?

It's easy to believe the enemy will only show up in our lives in big conspicuous ways with plenty of warning so we can get prepared for the attack. Reality doesn't play out like that. The enemy disguises himself in places like our thoughts.

Do you know why the thirty-day Klove challenge made such a difference in my life? A large part of it was shifting what I fed my mind. Going from constant messages of pain, loss, hopelessness, listlessness, apathy, anger, or hate to life, joy, promises that outlast our lifetimes, promises that give us strength and direction for our steps, hope, and peace. The difference is beyond night and day.

And that slowly helped me change how I defined my savior. The harder life gets, the more we're driven toward *something*. These repeat trials are helping me realize I'd been calling my trench my savior. Because the things I used down there helped me feel better in the moment, and I mislabeled the temporary relief as the ultimate end destination regardless of the particular problem.

In fact, the things that I can obtain quickly—all sorts of drugs, instant hits, fleeting intimacy—none of it really fills or heals anything. Those are lies of false progress and fleeting relief that help us feel like we're beating our trial because we feel lighter in the moment, and in those moments we can pull the shade to the larger picture of our lives and pretend everything's fine. Then that moment bleeds into the next, and before you know it, this is life now.

The truth about that shade is that it hides more than just the things we want to block out. It hides the way out. Don't get me wrong, that path will offer all the temporary relief you want. We can all choose to live a decade under the influence or more. But every single time, when the high wears off, it's back to the very reality you put so much effort into trying to avoid.

So maybe the things I can get quickly through my own effort aren't really worth the effort at all. Their end result always just brings me right back to the beginning I started at before I chose to pick them up. They're just a reset back to level one.

I am so sick of level one.

Just because my reality didn't change even slightly a day, a month, or a year after I've been praying for change doesn't mean change isn't coming. It doesn't mean my cry for help was ignored. It doesn't mean I'm not deeply loved, cared for, and looked after just because I didn't receive what I want and think I need the moment I asked for it.

My newfound resentment for level one helped me turn down a midweek party so I could go to small groups instead. And then it started feeling a little easier to turn down a weekend party here and there. And then slowly I just start turning down everything that I know there'll be hard drugs at, or even the possibility of that kind of temptation in my life.

It's strange at first, but that conviction I was feeling before lost all of its nasty, guilty aftertaste and slowly started morphing into a genuine desire to start turning these things down. To trade coke for calm, chaos for clarity, hangovers for heaven's focus. To give up what used to be my utopia because there is actually something better.

The longer I stay committed to these groups and become more open with sharing things that used to be tucked away in a hidden box called shame, the easier it gets not to feel guilty at all that part of me still desires the things I used to love. To my delighted surprise, this is actually normal. This is like a thing that everyone deals with. Not necessarily all the hard drugs in the world but the struggle to shake things that are bad for us and stop denying the basic need for help.

Do you know what that means? It means I don't have to feel ashamed. It means shame actually has no home here. It's like a continuation of the feeling I got that first Sunday when everything came rushing to the surface just to be carried away. It's like the deeper into it all that I get, the more all the toxic things in my life are released.

Its helped me start to look at everything just a little bit differently again. Now on the drive into work, in between tears at first, I choose to speak promises over my life. For months every day on my drive in, on my lunch break, on my drive home, and often several times in between, I just repeat to myself, "So let's not get tired of doing what is good. At just the right time we will reap a harvest of blessing if we don't give up."[25]

Sure, right now there's still no end in sight over my situation. But this is not forever. And what those two sentences represent are encouragement and a promise of favor that inspires new strength to carry on even when you're thrown straight into the middle of a hurricane on a desert island. Because when you don't give up, there's blessing waiting for you. That is a promise.

That promise gives strength to keep fighting, to progress to the next season, to not just lie down and take it, but to push back on the darkness.

Don't get me wrong here, it's all still work. Much like finding a therapist, there were several small groups I attended for a semester or more before I finally found the one that was where I needed to be. Unlike the different corridors of the trenches, there's not actually anything bad that happens when you go around exploring all your possibilities here. This is the right place to exude your energy because even if you do, you leave feeling filled up anyways. There's not really a down side. Incredible, right?

So I push on. Now that I have enough clarity not to feel guilty and broken because a temptation got the best of me at a vulnerable time in life, mixed with a solid support system if I need it thanks to an extended season of healthy relationship building, it gets easier to keep the distance between my trench and me, well, distant.

It's also getting easier to begin to define who I actually am. Most of my life I've used words like accident, unwanted, outcast, useless, and valueless. I never understood how to adopt a healthier version of any of that or how to even begin to think or speak a different narrative. Being planted is helping me to begin to use the right words to define myself. Words like beloved, valued, redeemed, even blessed. It feels weird for a while even just thinking those words about myself. So foreign. But when I think about the price that was paid so I could think and eventually speak those words over myself, the price is what makes that all possible. It leaves me thankful beyond description and helps me walk in a confidence that's greater than my own.

Although it did not happen instantly, several very long months after I've been really learning and embracing redefining myself and relentlessly seeking out good and healthy life choices, it finally did happen. I did not grow tired of doing good, and now the blessing is here! I finally have an interview lined up. At a Christian nonprofit, of all places. From bartending and Spencer Gifts to ministry. You definitely could have fooled me that this was the direction my life was going to take.

I go for the first interview and crush it. Obviously. The second and final interview is in just a couple days. I pray for all sorts of confirmation that this is the right next step for me to take, and receive every answer I'm after.

Another Monday rolls around, the day before my second interview, and something truly shocking goes down. The jackal has announced her resignation. The company is floored. We were all convinced after twelve years down she was just going to continue here until death, mercilessly destroying all new life in her path. But it's over. It's over, and my second interview is still in just under eighteen hours.

The company president calls me late that night well after I'm already home. It's a victory call of sorts. Like we'd survived a war together and somehow managed to come out the other side. There's new hope. Change will finally start to happen. The entire office and company atmosphere will be different forever from this point forward. It's finally over.

I'm thankful I had already asked for confirmation before this moment because it would be really easy to get swept up in the emotion and throw my opportunity away.

The good news doesn't erase my countless efforts at change and ignored pleas for help. I'm glad when I leave that it will be better for the ones who come after me, don't get me wrong. But I'm not about to pretend the egregious neglect can suddenly be swept under the rug now that the main offender is leaving. I am going to this interview in the morning and accepting this position when they offer it to me.

And that's exactly what happened. I spend my final two weeks training my replacement and doing my best to firm up the fragile foundation of that place before I leave.

Icing on the cake time, my brother is also back to doing pretty well. Getting healthy again and staying the heck away from ICUs and the things that get someone there.

Things all around are finally looking up.

So why is this chapter still going?

I took all my baby steps in the right direction. I didn't give up, the blessings came, level one has been moved on from. Time to progress, time for the next. Chop-chop.

Yeah. So the thing is sometimes we're really ready to move on. But sometimes we get thrown back into challenges because we haven't learned everything we need to yet. Level completion: 94 percent out of 100 percent. Retry.

Annoying? Yes. Painful? Yes. Difficult, challenging, burdensome? Yes. Unfair? Well, honestly it really depends on how you choose to look at it.

I started my new job the day after New Year's. Working at a nonprofit is very different from every other job I've had in life. Working for something that's technically a ministry adds another level to that. I learned a thoughtful question I should have asked in my interview is, "How much debt is your 501c3 carrying?" Had I known that number was over a million dollars, it probably would have altered my prayers a smidge. And also my reality.

I learn by week two, paycheck number one, that I have left the realm of the world where paychecks on paydays are guaranteed, or likely. Why would they hire someone they knew they couldn't pay? How does a million dollars in debt even happen? Why wouldn't someone say at, oh, I don't know, a hot $300,000 that maybe better decisions should start being made? And why wasn't that idea revisited at $500,000 or $900,000 of accumulated debt? I have so many questions.

My thirtieth birthday is next month, and this really isn't how I wanted to celebrate that. Still paying off the car debt, I really would like that security of getting paid for all the waking hours I work.

I don't understand. I mean I prayed over this extensively. I sought advice extensively. I even got confirmation that this was the right move—extensively! Why did he move me from security, from a place that was *finally* jackal-free, to this? Would it all have played out easier for me if I left God out of this decision? It really is starting to look like that. Or is this another enemy tactic?

I'd love to have some calm moments at home to try to figure that out, but this is not a season of smooth seas. I know couples have hard times, but we've been in therapy together for several months now, and things seem to continue to be on a steady decline. My thirtieth comes and goes, and the memory of that night is forever stained with a moment that was the beginning of the end.

Now instead of wedding plans, I'm looking for a new place to live, alone. Everything that's been invested into this relationship for years is now just meaningless. It couldn't have even lined up with the lease expiration on this apartment. There are still months to go living in a shell of shattered dreams with a love that has become unrevivable.

Now we're dividing up what we've built together, physically and emotionally, trying to figure out who gets the couch, the kitchen table. Accepting the fact that I'll soon be ripped away from pets on top of a person and a life that I desired, searched for, and toiled over for so long. It's just over. Just like that.

Even if you can see it coming, that fact takes away no pain whatsoever. It's all deeply gutting and consuming. The grief seems to come in heavy and hard, like tidal waves. One moment it feels like I'm finally regaining a bit of footing only to be hit again with a new realization of another level of loss. It's not just the death of a relationship. It's a burying season of so many dreams we'd cultivated together for five, ten years down the road. A lifetime of plans are now just dust and ash.

This will be the first time I've lived somewhere with only myself. How am I supposed to do this when I'm openly told twice every month that I might not get a paycheck? This was supposed to be a time of victory and celebration. Instead it's turned into the least secure I've ever felt.

I'm beginning to realize I've been defining my worth by being able to say I'm in a relationship, that someone loves me. Unhealthy but true. And just or not, that's adding a good deal of weight to the levels of grief I'm trying desperately not to spiral into.

A couple of months go by, and the time finally comes for actual moving out to happen. It's both a relief and a fresh blow of deep heartache. I come home, and the only things left are mine. For the first time, there's the silence of no pets and no other life here. I'm forced to live in this apartment, these remains of our dead life for a few more weeks. All I can do is cry when I'm here.

I get the news that my brother is back in the ICU. *If* he makes it out this time, there won't be another opportunity to end up back there. He is on the verge of death.

The sorrow of this season is becoming unbearable. My chest feels heavy when I breathe, all the time. I don't even know how to pray. Why is it all snowballing like this? Weeks go by, and it takes everything in me just to make it through the day so I can get home and cry. The pain is deeply crippling, overwhelming, and unrelenting.

The day for my own move finally comes, into my own studio apartment. At least I can pay my rent on a credit card here, so even if I don't continue to see paychecks, I can just destroy my credit and remain living with a roof over my head. I'm not great at silver linings right now.

I don't know if all studio apartments are like this or if this is a Pittsburgh unique feature, but the doorways are ever so slightly more narrow than a standard frame. One morning while I was rushing around trying not to be late, I took the corner too fast. That extra couple inches I'd spent a lifetime growing accustomed to having in my doorways became deeply missed in an instant. I'm on the floor when I realize I've momentarily blacked out and am in an outrageous deal of physical pain. I smashed my foot into the plaster rounding the corner, and I'm quite certain I've broken it.

Great time to live on the fourth floor of a building that has no elevator, and work on a second floor of another building that also has no elevator. Just, why? It's not even a good story, and this is going to take weeks to heal. Could one more thing even go wrong right now?

I'm at work about two weeks after this, and my cell phone rings. It's my doctor's office. I was just there a few weeks ago. Do they have a sixth sense that I've developed a purple appendage? Is this a sign that I should seek medical treatment for this? It's definitely setting a record for how long I've ever gone living with a purple foot. It is a bit alarming to look at. I know there's not much they can do for it besides charge me hundreds of dollars to tell me that fact, so I've been opting out.

I spend too long getting lost in my debating and the throbbing, and the call goes to voicemail. It really does hurt a lot. I wonder why they called? The voicemail is nondescript with a request to return the call. I call back and get the right person. She starts by taking a deep breath.

Why is she taking a deep breath?

She reminds me of the standard procedure that happened at my last appointment and that they ran standard tests like always. Why did she take a deep breath though? This call feels like it's lasting forever.

She continues to tell me the reason for the call is because one of the standard old tests they do every year came back with a non-standard result. I have to go back in so they can run another test to confirm if I've developed cancer or not.

God, why?

NOTHING ELSE MATTERS

*Without a vision, you cannot differentiate between what
is important and what is merely a distraction.*
—Michael Hyatt

I HAVE TO WAIT SIX WEEKS for the appointment. Will this be the year I die? At least my brother made it to rehab, so our family would only get hit once, in theory.

Six weeks is a long time. Surely if it was severe they would have done something to get me in sooner? I don't know if that's how it works or not. Or maybe it's so severe that time won't matter, and the additional testing is just to confirm the inevitable end.

It's not as if I'm a stranger to the reality of death. This year is certainly heavily laced with its stench. It's just a really different experience when you try to choose it versus it choosing you.

I'm working to not jump to conclusions. There is also the possibility that everything will be just fine. I technically haven't been given odds yet, so shouldn't it be safe to assume it's at least fifty-fifty here? I don't know.

I do know I don't want to have to walk through this. Hasn't this year been hard enough? It feels so unfair on so many levels. Maybe it will just always feel unfair when death gets involved in any manner, no matter the time or situation. It always has in the past.

It just is not sitting right with me. So the story of my life is going to be I overcame depression, addiction, finally got my life on track just to experience loss, heartbreak, get cancer, and die? God, help me navigate why it feels unfair.

Maybe it really is just my time. Maybe the breakup was just meant to happen when it did so I wouldn't have to drag another person through the end with me. What if it was an act of mercy? We all reach the edges of our vignettes sooner or later. I know I can come up with theories every moment from now until my appointment, but none of them will offer anything solid to hold on to. What is there left to anchor to here? Every aspect of my reality, everything, is shaken. Health was one of the last things I had here in this current season.

It's not like I'm preparing to die in six weeks. But to have knowledge like this and do nothing to prepare myself now instead of when I might be on the front line would be extremely foolish. The time to form the battle plan isn't while you're getting shot at. It's now, during the calm.

Which is, of course, easier said than done. Especially when I can feel the tremors from the fringes of the storm start to rattle me up just enough to initiate draining my calm right away from me. It easily feels all-consuming when I let my guard down and spend too much time allowing my anxiety over this to feed my imagination of the possible outcomes. The beginnings of those moments can be so subtle. They just sneak right in.

From this point forward, as far as I can tell, I have basically two options. Option one, I can freak out. I can panic, get angry, feed resentment, become bitter, shut down, and give up. Or option two, I can press into my Savior.

I remember the time in my life where I used to believe pressing into Jesus wouldn't change anything. That it was a waste of time and effort, that it was even foolish. Yet even in those times, that undeniable pull for something more, something deeper, relentlessly burned and ached in me. That insatiable yearning that there's got to be *more*.

I know you have that hunger too. We all do. We all struggle and strive to create meaning and value in and with our lives. To fill in any sort of reason as to why we're here. We look for things we can be part of, things that can define a larger picture of who we are, things that can provide a sense of identity and belonging for us.

I've already picked substances. Just about every last one of them. I've already picked getting wrapped up in relationships. Those all provided a way for me to bring perceived value into my life and the lives of the people around me. Because with those things, I could at least provide a temporary good time. I could bring in some sense of happiness to myself and others. It was just such an ever-revolving losing chase. It's all so fleeting, and at the end of the day, it ultimately just depletes who you are.

Those things just destroyed the formation of my identity instead of helping me build it. I'd watch these things carry bits and pieces of me away as swiftly as I'd reintroduce any of it right back in. And they all always ended the same way. Always leaving me at the very place I'm trying to escape, always leaving me to start on empty the next day.

What value is left from any of that to hold me up now, at a time when I need it the most? What foundation was built from any of the time spent running to things that never had any lasting roots? There's nothing left from them, and they were never enough. That surely isn't going to magically change now. All panicking and freaking out is going to do is drive me right back to all of that.

I am not going back. Because things are different this time. I have tasted, I have seen glimpses in my life of what can happen when I choose to run to the right Savior, the true Savior. I've seen what can happen when you choose a relationship—not drugs, not alcohol, not people, not money, not religion, not accomplishments or success or status or anything else—but a real relationship with Him.

He changes everything.

I choose to "remember today what you have learned about the Lord through your experiences with him. It was you who had these experiences. You saw the Lord's greatness, his power, his might."[26] I have seen firsthand how life can change when I focus on the relationship that matters the most. Remembering what I've come through, and how I got through, is what will help get me through this next battle.

"Up to this point the Lord has helped us."[27] That's a promise I can say has definitely already been seen in my life many, many times already. So why would he just randomly stop now? "God is not a man, so he does not lie. He is not human, so he does not change his mind. Has he ever spoken and failed to act? Has he ever promised and not carried it through?"[28] No. And in fact, "his faithful promises are your armor and protection."[29]

One of the hardest disconnects I've had to push through over the past several years is being able to learn and apply the promises to my life specifically. It's been so hard not to get stuck on the lie that none of these truths actually apply to me personally. Here I am again presented with the choice to continue to believe these truths or call it all a sham and go back to my trench.

And here is where the enemy is going to come back in with raging force. Here is where the lies are going to start again. "That's nice for the people who get to receive that, but not for you. Not for the outcast, the reject, the addict, the one who's done all these things and is too far gone now. The one who deserves this new trial because of what you've done." Don't let the lies negate the truth. Remember we have to "be careful what you think, because your thoughts run your life."[30]

Just because a feeling or a thought comes into your mind does not automatically make it true. That's why we're told to accept the help that's out there, to replace our thinking with truth[31] and, "let God transform you into a new person by changing the way you think."[32] "Letting your sinful nature control your mind leads to death. But letting the Spirit control your mind leads to life and peace."[33] I want life. And peace through it. Who wouldn't?

Could it be possible that this massive challenge I'm potentially about to face isn't really that big at all? Maybe it's secretly a series of baby steps in disguise. And maybe some of the most important steps we can take are taking the time to see what our Savior has to say about us. To build our foundation on something that cannot be shaken even when everything else is. To get to a place where we can say, "Even if I am attacked, I will remain confident."[34] Confident that even though this trial feels way bigger than what I can handle, that I don't have to handle it alone or with only my own strength.

Yet my mind immediately returns fire with a fresh weight of worthlessness. Who am I that I should feel confident? Who am I that I should deserve anyone to come fight on my behalf? "What is man that you are mindful of him, and the son of earthborn man that you care for him?"[35] This is frontline warfare. This isn't the time to be surprised by the blowback that comes in that will try to stop forward progress; it's the time to expect it.

It's easy to glaze over the details God tells us and choose the lies of the enemy's omissions. But the middle of the hurricane isn't the time to abandon him. It's the time to cling tighter. Identify the lie (worthlessness), then keep looking for the rest of the promise. "Yet you have made him a little lower than God, and you have crowned him with glory and honor."[36]

We are so precious to God. When he looks at us, his thoughts toward us are, *This is my beloved son,*[37] *my beloved daughter, my child.* Jesus paid the price so God can see us the exact same way he sees Jesus. Whole, complete, lacking nothing, deeply, deeply loved. The enemy will always try to make you forget and hide these vital, incredible, life-changing details from the forefront of your mind. The enemy knows that over time, that truth can work into the foundation of your identity and make it strong and unshakable, so that's one of the first things he goes after. We identify with and as the enemy when we speak his thoughts, his lies, his omissions over ourselves. We have to fight that.

The truth is that God loves us. Our identity is in him. He lovingly wraps around us in the depths of our sorrows and trials, and with you in mind, he extends the invitation to "give your burdens to [Him], and he will take care of you."[38]

God "takes no pleasure in making life hard, in throwing roadblocks in the way."[39] And when we're in a state of distress, He "hears his people when they call to him for help. He rescues them from all their troubles."[40] He "helps the fallen and lifts those bent beneath their loads."[41] He "is merciful and compassionate, good to everyone. He showers compassion on all his creation."[42]

His love is the foundation that changes everything. Because in it and through it, every fear, every burden, every emotion and feeling that threaten to overcome us are met by the overcomer. And he's not surprised by the battle you're about to face. In fact, he's told us that "I have equipped you for battle."[43]

We can trust that "the Lord always keeps his promises; he is gracious in all he does."[44] He tells us "when they call on me, I will answer; I will be with them in trouble. I will rescue and honor them."[45] Because of that, "they do not fear bad news; they confidently trust the Lord to care for them."[46]

Here's the truth—whether it's in six or twelve weeks, or another decade or another fifty years, I'm still going to die one day. You will too. We all will. So if I decide to make it my goal to work toward living forever down here just for living's sake, I'll still be disappointed one day when that impossible goal fails and death takes this body. After all, "you do not know what tomorrow will bring. What is your life? For you are a mist that appears for a little time and then vanishes."[47]

It's not a bad goal to want to live a long and healthy life, but it's not the ultimate achievement. You don't secretly win another one hundred years alive if you make it to or past a certain point. So if working toward a goal to see old age just to say you've lived a long and happy life is misguided steps, then what matters? What's the point of all of this?

You know, for so long I believed my life was just a stream of unfortunate and terrible events. I struggled for so long to understand or find any value or meaning in all this. But when I look back on it now, even when I'm potentially facing death, again, I can see the traces of God's goodness laced in all those terrible moments, in every chapter of my life.

What I was searching for was anything to fill the void, regardless of what season I was in. And when I look back, he was always there. Always waiting to speak to me when I cried out in desperation. Always extending his hand to me, just waiting for me to reach back out and take it. He never met me with judgment or disgust or any level of shame. Those were labels I added, labels broken, hurting people cast out because that's what they wanted to see, because those were the lies they chose to believe. And I got sucked right up in it with them. But that is not his heart.

What I should have called it was separation from true love. Even in the heart of the deepest days of my addictions, God never gave up on me. He never once looked at me and thought of me as a lost cause, he never saw me as too far gone. Not for a minute was I ever hopeless in his eyes. Just lost. The pull in me for something more was always him calling out to me, his beloved, to lead me back to him and all that he is.

The setup I thought my family was working in cahoots against me to get me "religious" again was actually them listening to the pull from love itself to urge their kid to come home. From the coin flip that I let decide my move, to those little old ladies, to a random bridge of a song that ultimately fueled my hunger to find a place where I could finally have a real encounter with God—it wasn't a setup working against me. Yes, it was hard and scary at times, but that setup changed my life. It changed who I am. That setup was the start of the way out of the trenches. He used it all, and he used it for good.

What I learned to control was where I needed to keep my focus. To "set our eyes not on what we see but on what we cannot see. What we see will last only a short time, but what we cannot see will last forever."[48] And even when it feels dark, we know that "I will give you treasures hidden in the darkness—secret riches. I will do this so you may know that I am the Lord, the God of Israel, the one who calls *you* by *name*."[49] After all, He told us "I would not have told the people to seek me if I could not be found."[50] He's not hiding from us. We're the ones who control where we look.

What I learned to break off was the pull I let the enemy keep on my mind over the narrative of my life. To reject the lies that come in and try to convince me that because life is hard that God's not there or he doesn't care or he's not good. The presence of trials or loss absolutely does not mean the absence of God or his goodness. In fact, we can "walk through the Valley of Weeping, [and] it will become a place of refreshing."[51] And there, in the valley of weeping we "go from strength to strength."[52] It's a place where we can get stronger. How? Because "I have given you authority to trample on snakes and scorpions and to overcome all the power of the enemy; nothing will harm you."[53] Our snakes and scorpions are things like addictions or heartbreak or loss or fill in the blank. We have been given everything we need to be victorious over all those things. Because "the Lord is the strength of his people, a fortress of salvation"[54] at exactly every single moment we need him, if we'd just press into him.

What I needed to learn to do when I was down was reach up to my comforter for help. Down and out will never be a description over my life ever again. "God is able to bless you abundantly, so that in all things at all times, having all that you need, you will abound in every good work."[55] Loss cannot steal that from you, and neither can disease. So even when I have to walk through those things, I can still be blessed abundantly. And by his strength through the trial, I will still have everything I need to accomplish the reason he allowed me to come here.

The baby steps I learned to take was listening to his voice and amplifying that louder than anything and everything the enemy was hurling at me. We will always be able to find a reason to be angry or bitter at the circumstances of life. You can choose to only look at what the enemy is doing and saying and live your life as your very own jackal, claiming victimhood as your captor. You can choose to only listen to his lies and mislabel them as your personal truths. Or you can choose to believe the promises. "When life gets really difficult, don't jump to the conclusion that God isn't on the job. Instead, be glad that you are in the very thick of what Christ experienced. This is a spiritual refining process, with glory just around the corner."[56]

The truth is that your trench is never just about the circumstance in front of you. It can be easy to get sucked into the tunnel vision trenches impose on us. Quite literally, they are just an upside-down tunnel anyways. The ultimate design of the trench is not to take you out. It's to expose the truth that you can't do this on your own, that you can't be your own savior.

The trenches are not the be-all and end-all. They're just another thing that can be used by him to reinforce the truth that we need more than what we're able to procure with our own hands. They don't have to be the conveyor belt pulling you to your end. Instead, they can be vessels of glory that are the first place his light tunnels into you. "Because of God's tender mercy, the morning light from heaven is about to break upon us, to give light to those who sit in darkness and in the shadow of death, and to guide us to the path of peace."[57]

The story of my life isn't just to look at all the trials I've overcome or to get stuck on the potential new trial creeping up over my horizon. The real story of this whole journey is to point to Jesus and say, "Look at what he brought me through! Look at how he never left my side for a single moment and at the deepest depths I've ever been. Look at how faithfully he kept revealing Himself to me. Look at how he was always the source of that contagious joy I'd spent my lifetime trying to find—especially through the trials. Look at how he can fill every void."

For so long, I let the darkness of the trenches mask the evidence of his love. Of how far before me that love began, how far it's come since that beginning, how it's always been constant, and still, it'll continue on long after me, far more than I yet have the ability to comprehend. And what his infinite love did was lay itself down so I didn't have to, so we don't have to. That love gave everything. Everything at the highest cost possible, for you and for me.

That love is Jesus. Jesus was God's love letter, sent for *you*. Jesus experienced everything we have.

"We do not have a High Priest who is unable to sympathize and understand our weaknesses and temptations, but One who has been tempted, knowing exactly how it feels to be human, in every respect as we are. [So] let us with privilege approach the throne of grace, that is, the throne of God's gracious favor, with confidence and without fear, so that we may receive mercy for our failures and find His amazing grace to help in time of need, an appropriate blessing, coming just at the right moment."[58]

For a long time, maybe a large part of me really didn't want to see it. I didn't understand how to believe it could possibly be true or be true for me personally. But the only reason I made it out of those trenches to tell the story is because his love came pouring in and invaded my darkness. His light was what I would keep getting glimpses of every time I thought it was going to be over. His endless mercy is what never stopped following me, picking me up every time I fell. His faithful goodness is what always went before me to sustain me, to guide me, encourage, strengthen, and protect me when I'd need it most.

How though? How is that possibly true? How can that be real? Especially if you're someone who's lived a life or portions of your life in places like I have. In places where you're relentlessly bullied, belittled, cast aside, labeled as valueless, worthless, and useless. Places where your voice is constantly stifled even when you're crying and screaming out for help. How could such a polar opposite reality exist and exist waiting and ready for you to be part of it? How could there actually be not only help but help founded in love, waiting just for you?

I mean, "we can understand someone dying for a person worth dying for, and we can understand how someone good and noble could inspire us to selfless sacrifice. But God put his love on the line for us by offering his Son in sacrificial death while we were of no use whatever to him."[59]

He knew that this was not going to be an easy ride for us. That's why he showed up. "I have come into the world as light, so that whoever believes in me may not remain in darkness."[60] He didn't come to get something from us or so he'd be able to hold this over our heads, making impossible demands for us to try to meet or repay. His motivator was love and compassion and you and me.

Just because you haven't been able to see another person in your life act from a position of unconditional love with no ulterior motive does not mean that it cannot or does not exist. That is a direct lie from the enemy to stop you from putting your guard down. If you have any amount of time invested in trying to hold that wall up, you know how exhausting it gets. The good news is you don't have to keep holding that wall up another day. You can choose to let it down, to rest and receive the best gift that exists. It's totally free, and there are no strings attached. Really.

God tells us, "My grace is all you need."[61] "For by grace you have been saved through faith. And this is not your own doing; it is the gift of God."[62] And "to all who did receive him, who believed in his name, he gave the right to become children of God."[63]

As his kids, we inherit his gifts. It is for you personally. "Your Father knows what you need even before you ask,"[64] so he went ahead of you to make sure you would always have everything you would ever need to not only face but come out the champion in every struggle, every battle, every hardship, every loss, every heartache, in absolutely everything you will face in this lifetime that feels harder or bigger than what you can handle.

"God will strengthen you with his own great power so that you will not give up when trouble comes, but you will be patient."[65] Patient in knowing that even though you may still have to walk through the hard thing that you can't see a way out of yet, you will be met there with not only strength but everything else you need to make it through. He is faithful, and he is coming to meet you right there where and when you need him the most.

All that to say the ultimate goal of our lives shouldn't be just to make it to a certain age, a certain retirement goal, or list of accomplishments along the way. Those things are great, don't get me wrong, but at the end of the line, if you look back and those are the only things you have to stand on, you've missed it. Because the ultimate goal, the ultimate achievement to strive after in our time here isn't to accumulate what we can't take with us when our time in this life is over.

The real goal, the biggest win we can ever accomplish in our time in these bodies, is to know him. To have relationship with him. To surrender our will to him. That surrender is not a loss, quite the opposite.

Do you know what *my* desires are in the face of trial? They're things I used to know, things I used to be comfortable with. So if I were to keep living right now without surrendering my will and desires, I'd inevitably reach a point where I could convince myself I'm dying soon, so I might as well go back to stimulants full-time in order to maximize the amount of hours I'm awake in the time I have left. I'm no doctor, but safe to say there's nothing about elevating my heart rate and staying awake for three to four days at a time that would elongate my life. In fact, it would do exactly the opposite. So what about surrendering that is a bad thing? Nothing.

All surrender is not bad. Surrendering to him is actually life-giving. Because you can surrender your sorrow and trade it for his joy. You can surrender your despair and worry and trade it for his peace. You can surrender your confusion and trade it for the certainty that he's not going to lead you astray. You can surrender your emptiness and trade it for fullness in all that you lack. You can surrender your hard heart, your wall, your coarse voice from crying out in your pain to the things that could never save you and trade it for his mercy to come rushing to meet you exactly where you are right now.

Most importantly, you can surrender your eternity in separation from him and trade it for eternity in his presence, where the fullness of joy will forever be. Where you will be complete, lacking nothing, in a place that won't be home to pain or loss or sorrow ever again. "I give them eternal life, and they will never perish. No one can snatch them away from me."[66]

How can it be true? Because he told us it is, and his word does not return void.[67] And the more you surrender to him, the more you get to know him, the more he proves to you and shows you how true and trustworthy his promises are again and again.

So how does any of this help me if I might be facing cancer in the eye? Obviously, if I end up with a positive diagnosis, the goal would be to do what I need to do to beat it. But what if beating it is not an option?

I used to be trapped under this mentality that said if I'm the only one who's making an effort, then it's not worth the effort at all. Looking back, I can see other people's obedience cast out acting as my life lines. Those little old ladies had no idea their act of obedience was going to topple the first domino of change in my life. He uses all of it to go after the one who's lost. So if that's what he's doing through this trial for someone else, and it's my turn to cast out the life line, then I'm going to decide, before I might go into this season, what my endgame is.

I will make the effort to stay faithful, even if no one else around me is. I will make the effort to put on joy, even if I have to walk through chemo. I will make the effort to trust that through this suffering, I will be supported, strengthened, and restored, whether that is on this side of the grave or the next. I will choose faith, even if the outcome isn't the one I want.

Yes, one of the goals will be to beat this trial if I end up having to face it. But that is absolutely not the ultimate end goal. The real goal will be reflecting him and sharing his promises in every step along the way. We're designed to be filled with joy so much that we overflow with hope.[68] It's not a flippant "oh, I hope this or that happens" kind of hope. It's a confident trust that what he said is true, and letting that truth be the driving force behind what keeps us going.

This is our hope. "Day by day the Lord takes care of the innocent, and they will receive an inheritance that lasts forever. They will not be disgraced in hard times."[69] "He [has already] lifted me out of the slimy pit, out of the mud and mire; he set my feet on a rock and gave me a firm place to stand."[70] I have already seen him work in my life, on my behalf. His promises were true then, and they're true now. So when fear about what's going to happen to my future comes, I can fight it with more of his promises. "Fear not, for I am with you. Do not be dismayed. I am your God. I will strengthen you; I will help you; I will uphold you."[71]

He will help you. You might be staring something terrifying in the face right now, but he's right there with you, and he's bigger than whatever you're facing. When it starts to feel like it's going to take you out, cry out to him. "How gracious he will be when you cry for help! As soon as he hears, he will answer you."[72]

Even if "weeping may last for the night, there is a song of joy in the morning."[73] That's a promise. This is the hope that I am choosing now that I will continue to declare over my life. This is what I choose to have flowing out of me. Even if it's hard, even if I'm nearing the end, these are the truths that have not, do not, and will not change.

The fear, the hardship, the weeping—none of it has the final say. He does. And in the end, he wins. And if we're his kid, we win. The victory is ours. Even if it looks dark for a season, even if the road looks different than we thought it would, even if it hurts more than we ever expected, in the end we win.

When the enemy comes to try to rob that confidence, fight him. Lean on Jesus, press into his promises for you. He's not leaving you. He says, "I am with you always, to the very end of the age."[74] If we just trust that, trust him, believe him, he "will keep him in perfect peace whose mind is stayed on you, because he trusts in you."[75]

That peace is ours. It's yours to claim, to own, to live, to feel.

"Don't worry about anything, but pray [aka just talk to Him] about everything. With thankful hearts offer up your prayers and requests to God. Then, because you belong to Christ Jesus, God will bless you with peace that no one can completely understand. And this peace will control the way you think and feel."[76] It's about deciding, choosing to trust everything to him, and what we get in return is peace.

Commit means to pledge or bind.[77] We can commit our thoughts, we can bind them to Jesus. We can bind our uncertainties and fears and anxieties to him. We're told to "commit everything you do to the Lord. Trust him, and he will help you."[78] Do you know what binding a burden to him does? It frees you. When it's bound to him, it's off of you. He doesn't just take the burden and the leave a void. He takes it and replaces the void of your burden with his presence. And he can't wait to do this for you! This is the essence of his character. To always be everything you need in every moment you have need.

He first gave us his Son to provide us the opportunity to live eternity with him when this life is over. He could have stopped there, but he didn't. "He who did not spare his own Son but gave him up for us all, how will he not also with him graciously give us all things?"[79] This is the heart, the core, the identity of who he is. Provider, sustainer, life-giver, healer, Savior, fortress, shield, our hope no matter what comes, no matter what we face.

Knowing this is what really matters. And believing it changes everything.

Knowing this makes me confidently say that even if I face a trial in the next few weeks where I'll be forced into a position of fighting for my life, my hope will absolutely not be shaken.

I choose to bind the fear to him, to commit it to him. And even if my own life is the one that's lost, I refuse to go out without at least trying to take the only thing with me to heaven that I possibly can.

I need you to know that "everyone who calls on the name of the Lord will be saved."[80] This truth, this salvation, these promises are all for you. The way out of the trenches is here. It's him.

The real story of my life is that "God had mercy on me so that Christ Jesus could use me as a prime example of his great patience with even the worst sinners. Then others will realize that they, too, can believe in him and receive eternal life."[81]

You just have to trust him first. It's okay if you don't know what to do after that. Just receive him, then he'll show you the rest as you go. "He delights in each step we take."[82] "You will show me the path of life; In your presence is the fullness of joy; In Your right hand there are pleasures forevermore."[83]

Cancer doesn't have the final say in how my story ends. He does.

Your trench doesn't have to have the final say in how your story ends. But you have to be the one who makes that decision.

You can make it right now, this very moment.

IT'S YOURS TO TAKE

*Life is 10 percent what happens to you and
90 percent how you react to it.*
—Charles Swindoll

IT'S NOT DARK AT ALL. What I wouldn't give for it to be dark right now. I have to settle for closing my eyes, but still the extra lights propped up around me for this procedure make it impossible to pretend I'm anywhere else.

I let my mind wander to the old story I've heard a thousand times starting from my childhood. This group of people were freed from years and years of slavery. God sent these straight-up crazy plagues all over the land until the unjust leader gave in and freed the slaves. Dude changed his mind in what seemed like mere hours and decided to send an army after them to get the slaves back in bondage. He felt played. But God's heart for the oppressed wasn't going to lose.

The slaves were, well, slaves. Not at all equipped to go out into the desert to wherever their freedom was waiting for them. Certainly not remotely equipped to fight an organized army. It wasn't long before they all knew they were being chased, and to say it was looking bleak would be the understatement of the century. Their trenches weren't just luring them back in, they were chasing after them.

Night began to fall, and they came to a sea. A sea. "Good thing we carried all these boats with us!" said no one ever. They were screwed. Darkness, a raging, angry enemy, a sea that may as well have been an ocean, and thousands of people filled with fear. As if a lifetime of slavery hadn't been enough already.

It would be easy to just let the voice from their past continue to define who they are. It would be easy to give up and let the army just take them back to their trench lives. It would even be easy to just walk into the sea. I'm sure it crossed some of their minds. An overwhelming feeling of being trapped from every angle, chased down just to be tortured again, to be beaten again, belittled, cast aside, labeled as far less than human. It would be so much easier just to let the water take you and let that life and everything else that life had to offer just end.

I'm sure every minute felt like an eternity. What could they possibly do at this point?

The truth is, there wasn't anything any of them could do. Except pray.

True story—you can read all about this.[84] This dude Moses takes, of all things, a stick. I guess a staff, if we're being technical, but it may as well have been a toothpick in a situation that dire to anyone looking in. He puts his li'l sticky stick right in the water, right in the sea.

In that moment, it was probably quite a gift that it was dark, it was nighttime. Can you imagine the comments that would have come out of the majority of the crowd? I know I would've had comments to vocalize about the sheer lunacy of the scene. Who would have thought that darkness would have been a gift in a moment where you're literally running blind running for your life?

But then the miracle. The sea split. Like a path of dry land was opened up right down the middle of a freaking sea. Like, are you kidding me? Then in a hurried rush, knowing they were still being chased, the flock of slaves ran right into the open path.

I imagine, had it been day, they all would have been able to see every living thing that was swimming in the sea. I imagine, if I was an aquatic something or other, I'd likely be a bit baffled as to how there were now two different surfaces when there had only ever been one. I imagine that curiosity would have drawn quite the crowd of aquatic life.

There are sharks in the Red Sea. Lots of them. In fact, a quick Google search[85] tells of forty-four different shark species and about a thousand different other species that no doubt would have been utterly terrifying to see face-to-face, with no glass, no container, and no emergency button for help to push in case the invisible wall collapses.

Can you imagine not only running for your life but doing so in the dead of night? Then somehow, a sea splits, and your only option is to walk into it. Okay, great, now can you imagine if it was daylight? You could have been looking countless sharks and plenty of other things that could still kill you right in the eye, not only once but nearly every step of the way. Can you imagine the added terror daylight would have brought in those moments?

The darkness was a gift. And sometimes the darkness is what is necessary for the miracle to be complete in all its glory.

I never would have thought of darkness as a gift before. I wonder what gifts of darkness I've mislabeled in my life as a curse, not knowing what I was frustrated I couldn't see was something that was actually going to terrify or paralyze me in fear. What I wouldn't give for the gift of darkness right now.

But it's blindingly bright in this procedure office. Strangely enough, it's just me and the doctor. I'm really surprised that there aren't other staff here, at least a nurse. The procedure starts, and although I'm told it will be pretty quick, it won't be painless or comfortable in any manner.

I take a deep breath and try to relax. Before I can even finish exhaling, the door of the room swings wide open. I jump, which is of course bad because the doctor has already started the procedure. It's a nurse who's entered the room, and she's clearly either late of her own volition or the last pick of the available staff, neither of which instills the slightest bit of confidence in me.

The doctor is clearly and verbally upset that I jumped at the sudden and unexpected outburst into the room. I apologize, not because I'm sorry but because the position I'm in is the definition of vulnerable, and I'd like to try to keep this stranger on my good side, at least until this is over.

I timidly ask if any other staff will be coming in the room to try to combat any more extremely valid jumps on my end. Instead of an apology from either staff for the rude and unannounced entry, I'm scolded, nearly yelled at to be still, and reminded this is not a simple procedure and that other staff was necessary.

I fight the urge to kick the doctor straight in the teeth with as much force as my entire being can muster. Which is a challenge. But I know an assault charge will not solve any of my problems here, and this is a "pick your battles" kind of moment. I don't have it in me to reschedule and wait another six weeks or longer just to go through it again. So I close my eyes and try to welcome as much darkness as I can because some roads really are just better traveled in the dark.

My mind is flooded with an old hymn that I didn't even know I still knew the words or melody to. What a shocking yet strangely calming surprise. I used to think old hymns were just cheesy choruses sung to repetitive piano, but that whole time I was wrong. Those are the heart cries of the victors who've gone before us to show us the way through. And now it's an unforeseen anthem to get me through these moments that feel like they're moving in slow motion. Unexpected comfort when I need it most, and a very present reminder that he's with me in this.

It finally ends, and thankfully, I make it to my driver seat and close my car door before I lose it. The culmination of all the heavy emotions is too much to keep in, so I sit there in the parking lot, crying. I never imagined the staff would be so rude through such an already challenging to walk through process.

I never thought this was what thirty was going to be like. Loss after loss followed by trial after trial, just one after the next with no rest in between. What on earth is this kind of darkness hiding from me? How is any of this a gift? I just can't see it. I just don't understand.

Father, help me.

I feel too heavy to do anything but go home. I call off the rest of the day at work before I leave the parking lot. I know it's only 10:00 a.m., but I buy a bottle of wine at a gas station before I make it home. The reality of walking into an empty apartment with this kind of weight feels like too much. I just feel so alone in this, and today I don't have the fight in me to be stronger than my old addiction.

I make it up the four flights of stairs into my four hundred square feet of home and put on a song that got me through my breakup. "Highs and lows / You surround me either way it goes / Should I rise or should I fall / Lord You're with me through it all."[86] The tears start again, motivated by pain but also by thankfulness for that promise.

The physical pain is present, but it pales in comparison to the war in my mind, the battle raging inside. Part of me wants to give up, to let this win just so it can end. The truth is that I'm tired of fighting. I feel like I have nothing left to give. The pain, again, feels deeply all-consuming, and the loneliness of this moment and this day and this trial is trying with all its force to encompass me. But that's why I put this song on.

Even though the reality of the pain feels true, the reality of the promise is true. Even though I feel lonely in this, I am not alone. He is with me. Even though the weight of all of this feels like it's too much to take, it feels like it's pushing me to the cusp of being completely consumed by the darkness it's bringing with it. It feels like it's going to push me off the edge. Even though that's all true, what's still true is that the darkness can be a gift.

I do not have to let those feelings win. I don't. The truth is that he surrounds me and this situation no matter how it goes. All those heavy, negative feelings are attacks. They're lies from the enemy trying to kick me when I'm vulnerable. But in this attack, I can choose to step behind his shield, into the shadow, the darkness of his protection.

Music is part of that shield, especially worship songs. It is truths to declare out loud, weapons in the battle, and protection for your mind and soul. Music is powerful, and we need powerful when the battle is raging and the enemy is right in our face, attacking.

Science backs that up.

> Sound is an incredibly powerful therapeutic tool. As quantum physics has shown us, the

entire universe is made up of vibrations. Sounds can help us tap into the resonant frequencies needed to heal disease by translating specific acoustic vibrations into meaningful neurological impulses that heal us, mentally, spiritually, and physically.[87]

I guess that's why I always found such comfort in music when I was a teenager. Music is serious weaponry. It can heal us, it can give us strength, it can remind us of what we forget to look at when we choose to make our problems larger than everything else. And I still have several days to wait for the test results. Heavy weaponry is welcomed right now. Needed, really. I need these promises on endless repeat. I need an endless loop that washes peace over my mental battle, because my peace threatens to leave by the minute.

So I choose to nestle myself into the darkness of his shield and let him fight for me. "The Lord will fight for you; you need only to be still."[88]

Waiting sucks. Being still during times of high stress is hard. I want to be doing something, preparing for everything I can, figuring out the next steps if I get hit with bad news when these results show up. But I don't have another option right now. There is nothing I can do to make the test results arrive any faster than they're going to. And this is yet another test of "what am I going to do? Am I going to freak out, or am I going to press into him in this darkness?"

"Highs and Lows" starts again because I literally have it on repeat. It pulls me back into my last apartment to the night I was sitting alone for the first time in it. I remember how dark that moment felt. The only thing that made it bearable, the thing that gave me strength to continue taking the next breath, was the strength and grace of God. He fought for me that night, and he is fighting for me right now.

What came out of the darkness of that breakup was my decision to start serving at church, to join the production team and help make services happen. The heaviness of that loss turned into fuel to continue to be part of something larger than myself. To step into being part of something that points people to the love of Jesus. Because that love is what got me through that darkness, period. It was all him. The gift of that darkness turned into a path of light. A path that, every week, has the potential to change someone's eternity. To change their every day, to show people his heart. That darkness was a gift, not only to me but now to everyone else who gets to meet him for the first time through the sacrifice I get to make every week through serving. I wouldn't have had the final push to give my time and my talent had it not been for the pain.

And even more than that, the pain and darkness of death held its own gifts. Even after I had just come back to God, and then got hit with the actual death of someone who was really supposed to out-live me. Somebody I would have married. Somebody I loved deeply. I had the opportunity to encourage a room full of strangers and some of my close friends through giving his eulogy. And I had the oppor-tunity to hand over my deeply shattered heart into the hands of the restorer for healing. The depth of my relationship with Jesus grew deep roots through that pain and formed the foundation I'm stand-ing on now through this pain. God was the answer then. He is the one who got me through that. He has done it time and time again and again, and he's going to be the answer now.

No matter what the test result is, the answer is him. No matter how dark it feels, his light will always find me and meet me. No mat-ter how much it hurts, he will heal me. I just have to be still, let him fight, and wait for the gift that is going to come out of this particular new darkness that is covering me right now. There are always trea-sures waiting for us, there is always hope through it, and redemption will always come. The promise is true that "after you have suffered a little while, he will restore, support, and strengthen you, and he will place you on a firm foundation."[89]

The darkness finally just drives me to him. What a gift that is since in him we truly have everything we will ever need.

I finally feel strong enough to let this song end its long ses-sion of playing on repeat. Focusing on him has flooded me with this unreal peace that I certainly cannot properly explain. I can honestly say I slept so well that night.

I spend the next few days praising him. My heart is strong, and though anxiety tries to creep back in on the regular, I combat it and smother it with worship. He has never failed me. That truth allows me to rejoice. And that is what I'm clinging to. I just want him and his presence. I want to "draw near to God and He will draw near to you."[90] How beautiful is that? He wants to be close to us as much as we'll allow. He is literally constantly just waiting to be invited in to your situation so he can make it better.

I should be worried right now, but my soul is at rest. I should be panicking and looking into different doctors and facilities while I'm waiting, but I'm full of hope. I should be losing sleep and having trouble eating because of anxiety, but I am full of joy. Even if the worst thing happens, my confidence remains that there is nothing that can separate me from him. And as long as I have him, nothing else matters because I will always have everything I need.

I didn't expect to become one of the people that first grew my curiosity. Someone who is able to be going through something hard and remain unshaken. Someone who has finally caught and embedded that contagious joy. I am so thankful for the trials, the pain, the trenches. He has shown me the gifts of darkness, and they have all ultimately pointed me to him. I wouldn't trade any of it because where I am now is incredible. Knowing him and being in relation with him has changed who I am to the core, and if this was the only way I ever would have gotten here, I would do it over and over again. Knowing him truly is *that* good.

I'm floating in this peace when the day finally comes. I'm sitting at work. It's about two o'clock in the afternoon, and I receive an email notification from my doctor's office. The test results are in.

A flood of adrenaline hits my brain like a line of cocaine. I can literally feel my pupils dilate and my heart jump from my chest to my throat down through my arms and out into the room. Whoever said sober life is boring lied to you. Plenty o' highs remain, let me tell you.

I debate if I should just look at it now or wait the two hours and forty five minutes until I'm home in a private space where I'm free to fall apart as needed.

What a strange place to be, sitting in and old administrative office of a Catholic school built in the early nineteen hundreds. The angry hornet who can never find his way out of my office buzzing above my head, endlessly pinging into the fluorescent light twelve feet above me. And me sitting here, in a chair probably just as old as I am, knowing a simple login to my UPMC app and the words that follow hold the results that are going to be either entirely life-changing in every aspect of the definition or a heavy weight lifted that everything's fine and life will continue on as normal.

Why am I here, of all places, for this moment? Why was I in a chocolate museum, of all places, along streets lined with stoplights topped with Hershey's Kisses when I got some of the worst news of my entire life? Life can be so strange.

I can't resist. If it's bad news, at least I will have people immediately around me to pray for me. A plus that makes the bimonthly question of "will I get a paycheck this time?" feel worth it. Maybe that's why I'm particularly right here right now.

I close my office door to the hallway and open the test results. It's a lot longer than I thought it would be, with a lot more medical jargon than I expected. I guess I thought it would just say "cancer" or "no cancer," but it's several long paragraphs of a lot of words I'm going to have to google.

I sigh and stop for a minute and debate just calling into the doctor's office. But do I really want to force a stranger into explaining something potentially awful to me just because it seems like a lot in this moment? That just doesn't feel fair to them. And Google exists, and I'm grown. Surely I can figure this out.

I continue reading where I left off, then I finally come to the part where it all makes sense, and I see a word that, had it been spoken over me years ago, would have really crippled my spirit. But now it's a word that's encouraging, and it floods me with joy and relief: *unremarkable.*

I feel weight lifting off me as I keep reading the rest of the results. More medical jargon followed by my new favorite word again—*unremarkable.* I continue on and see it a few more times—*unremarkable, unremarkable, unremarkable.* And just like that, it's over.

My entire being erupts in praise and tears. I text my family the good news so they can rejoice with me. I put on a worship song and just sit in this moment, giving thanks to Jesus.

I touch base with my doctor's office, and they confirm this is good news. I'll still have to go in annually to test, but they don't anticipate me being in this situation again down the road and the follow-up tests won't be nearly as unpleasant as this last one was.

Everything's all right. Just like that. Life can be so strange. It's not like it's a golden ticket that stops all possibility of me being in a situation where I might have to face something like this all over again. But for right now, everything's okay.

And even if I have to walk this road again, I know exactly what my game plan is going to be because it's already been developed and put in place through this trial. It will always be to run to and cling to him.

I've made it this far only because of him. I have hope for my future only because of him. I have strength through the trials because he gives me his. I've been gifted everything I'll ever need because he loves me. And until it finally is my time to leave this earth and go home to be with him, he'll continue to grace me with exactly what I need at exactly the moment I need it until my last breath.

This trial was a fresh reminder of all of that. And when the next one comes, whether it's tomorrow or next month or next year, all of the promises he's given me will continue to carry me through. The darkness will continue to refine and bring out his treasures. I just have to continue to trust.

I consider every moment from this one forward a gift. Gravy. I'm not yet sure why he chose to continue to keep me here, but I trust fully that I've got a purpose with the time I have left. And I have no doubt that as I continue to press into him, he will continue to guide me and reveal to me all he has waiting in this life that was meant just for me.

All I have to do is step into it and take it.

PS

As much in the same way as the story of my life is not that I beat addiction, beat depression, just to get cancer, go through loss and die, it's also not all of that plus—well, I didn't get cancer, so for everybody who's still out there in the middle of their trench, good luck! I'm signing off. It's not like that at all.

Because let's continue to be honest. I know there are some of you reading right now that are disappointed that this is how the story's about to end. That I didn't have to walk through that struggle. But you did. But you are. Or you're about to, because you just got your bad news just the other day.

That's why he sent me first, that's why he brought me through everything that he did with as much hope as I have now. Because I know it's not fair, and I know you don't deserve to be going through this, and I know it feels like you want to lash out at everybody and everything around you because this is hard. And you shouldn't have to be going through it. And I agree. I might not know your particular situation, but I agree that you absolutely should not have to be going through it. You shouldn't, it's not fair. And my heart breaks and bleeds and cries with you.

And that is exactly why God sent Jesus. Because he looks at you in this situation and says, "I know this is going to take you out of the body that you're in now, and that's going to be really scary, and that's going to be a trial that I never designed for you to go through. But I love you so much that I sent Jesus to make a way so that through this life and when this life is over, you have security and you have comfort and a never-ending hope and joy unspeakable waiting for you. Despite this hard thing."

So don't give up. Don't give up on that, don't give up on him. Because this world will always beat you down and wear on you until you feel completely hollowed out, wishing it would be over. For some of us, that's exactly how it's going to end, feeling just like that. *But it doesn't have to.* And we don't have to walk through this defeated.

We have the confident hope to walk out of this with our head held high, knowing that when we reach the next part of what our souls were designed for, of all that is waiting for us, it will dwarf all of the pain and the trials and the trenches in this life.

We don't have to be afraid of the journey there. Unfamiliar isn't always bad. And you're allowed to step into this for the first time skeptical. It's okay, it just gives him more opportunity to show off how good he is. Ask him to help you see him. "Ask the Lord your God for a sign."[91] You have the power in your life to decide to ask. And that little bit that we can actually control does have the power and ability to radically shift and transform the course of our lives.

Just because you haven't stepped into this yet doesn't mean the gateway to a life that holds more than you ever could have imagined isn't right there waiting for you. It's our own reluctancy to trust his plan for our lives and have faith that he is endlessly for us that's ultimately the only thing holding us back from true victory and advancement.

Some of us have lived with such hardened hearts for so long that we refuse to believe any of this has any possibility of holding any water, of being true in the slightest. It's absolutely never too late for you to change your mind, to finally surrender what you've been wrongly clinging to and what you can't control.

"The same Lord is Lord of all and richly blesses all who call on him, for, 'Everyone who calls on the name of the Lord will be saved.'"[92]

Had I known the truth of the leveling out of everything at the foot of the cross, had I understood the depth of compassion, the depth of a Father longing for his beloved to come home, regardless of anything that's happened, had I known that that kind of extravagant love overrides and overrules all of our human tiers of sin and offense, had I known and experienced the overwhelming passion poured out for me that smothers every judgment and prejudice that entered my life—had I just *known!* My trenches never would have been as dark or lasted as long as I let them. It would have given me the strength to get up and face the day when I had nothing left in me to get back up so much sooner in my life had I just known.

No matter what it looks like for you personally, we all have things in our past and in our present that constantly fight to be the loudest voice in what defines us. It's time to finally let that voice be his. You can become his, right now today. And you can receive the blessings and the benefits that follow as soon as you accept him. And it's really simple.

> "If you declare with your mouth, 'Jesus is Lord,' and believe in your heart that God raised him from the dead, you will be saved."[93]

It's as easy as saying "God, I know I'm a sinner. I know I can't do this on my own, and I know I can't be my own savior. I believe that Jesus came, died, and rose again, conquering death, hell, and the grave, and he did it just for me. I ask you to come into my life and into my heart. I've been forgiven, transformed, and healed, and it's all because of you. Be the Lord of my life. In Jesus's name, amen."

It might feel like the beginning of the end because it is, and that's a good thing even if in the moment it feels like you're stepping into the abode of madness with your decision. That's a sign you're on the right track. Keep going!

We should all reach a point in our lives where we look at it and don't recognize it as our own anymore—because now it's his. It's been healed, renewed, and transformed into something that is absolutely better than any and everything else that this world has to offer.

Your problems might not all magically vanish the moment you finish saying that. But don't be fooled—your life has absolutely changed in ways that are about to continuously blow your mind.

The God of the universe is fighting for you, and all of heaven is cheering you on. And even if it's still dark, know that "all that night the Lord drove the sea back."[94] He's making a way for you. He's working out a miracle for you. And he will get you through and out of your trenches.

It's all yours to reach out and take.

What are you going to choose?

NOTES

Call It What It Is

[1] History.com editors, "First trenches are dug on the Western Front," History, November 16, 2009, https://www.history.com/this-day-in-history/first-trenches-are-dug-on-the-western-front

[2] "World War I Trench Facts & Worksheets," KidsKonnect, March 1, 2019, https://kidskonnect.com/history/wwi-trenches/

[3] Praveen Anand et al., "Trench Foot or Non-Freezing Cold Injury As a Painful Vaso-Neuropathy: Clinical and Skin Biopsy Assessments," PubMed, September 29, 2017, https://pubmed.ncbi.nlm.nih.gov/28993756/

It's a Setup

[4] https://www.iwm.org.uk/history/voices-of-the-first-world-war-trench-life

[5] https://graphics.wsj.com/100-legacies-from-world-war-1/trench-warfare

[6] https://worldwaronetrenchwarfare.weebly.com/trench-warfare-in-world-war-1.html

What You Can Control

[7] https://www.smithsonianmag.com/history/legends-what-actually-lived-no-mans-land-between-world-war-i-trenches-180952513/

[8] Big Daddy Weave, "Redeemed."

Break Off What's Breaking You

9 https://www.longlongtrail.co.uk/soldiers/a-soldiers-life-1914-1918/life-in-the-trenches-of-the-first-world-war/
10 Hillsong Worship, "Love on the Line."

Using My Down to Push Me Up, Not Out

11 https://www.britannica.com/topic/air-warfare
12 A devotional from author Max Lucado
13 1 Corinthians 2:9

Baby Steps Are in Fact Still Steps

14 https://nami.org/get-involved/awareness-events/suicide-prevention-aware-ness-month
15 https://ourworldindata.org/suicide
16 https://www.nimh.nih.gov/health/statistics/suicide
17 https://www.thetrevorproject.org/survey-2021/?section=Introduction
18 https://www.samhsa.gov/suicide/at-risk
19 https://nami.org/get-involved/awareness-events/suicide-prevention-aware-ness-month
20 https://www.psychiatry.org/newsroom/news-releases/american-psychiatric-as-sociation-renews-call-to-action-after-dramatic-increase-in-overdose-deaths
21 https://www.who.int/news-room/fact-sheets/detail/opioid-overdose
22 https://www.forbes.com/sites/tommybeer/2021/03/03/self-harm-claims-among-us-teenagers-increased-99-during-pandemic-study-finds/?sh=fdc20e-a33e05
23 https://en.wikipedia.org/wiki/List_of_military_engagements_of_World_War_I
24 Psalm 116:1–13, 16–17 TPT
25 Galatians 6:9 NLT

Nothing Else Matters

26 Deuteronomy 11:2 GNT
27 1 Samuel 7:12 NLT
28 Numbers 23:19 NLT
29 Psalm 91:4 NLT
30 Proverbs 4:23 ICB

31 Derived from 1 Corinthians 13:11
32 Romans 12:2 NLT
33 Romans 8:6 NLT
34 Psalm 27:3 NLT
35 Psalm 8:4 AMP
36 Psalm 8:5 AMP
37 Matthew 3:17 NIV
38 Psalm 55:22 NLT
39 Lamentations 3:33 MSG
40 Psalm 34:17 NLT
41 Psalm 145:14 NLT
42 Psalm 145:8–9 NLT; also see Psalm 116:5 NIV
43 Isaiah 45:5 NLT
44 Psalm 145:13 NLT
45 Psalm 91:15 NLT
46 Psalm 112:7 NLT
47 James 4:14–15 ESV
48 2 Corinthians 4:18 NCV
49 Isaiah 45:3 NLT, emphasis added
50 Isaiah 45:19 NLT
51 Psalm 84:6 NLT
52 Psalm 84:7 NIV
53 Luke 10:19 NIV
54 Psalm 28:8 NIV
55 2 Corinthians 9:8 NIV
56 1 Peter 4:12–13 MSG
57 Luke 1:78–79 NLT
58 Hebrews 4:15–16 AMP
59 Romans 5:7–8 MSG
60 John 12:46 ESV
61 2 Corinthians 12:9 NLT
62 Ephesians 2:8 ESV
63 John 1:12 ESV
64 Matthew 6:8 CEV
65 Colossians 1:11 NCV
66 John 10:28 NLT
67 Isaiah 55:11 NKJ
68 Romans 15:13 MSG
69 Psalm 37:18–19a NLT
70 Psalm 40:2 NIV, my own words added
71 Isaiah 41:10 TLB
72 Isaiah 30:19 NIV
73 Psalm 30:5 GW

[74] Matthew 28:20 NIV
[75] Isaiah 26:3 ESV
[76] Philippians 4:6–7 CEV
[77] *Merriam-Webster*, "commit," https://www.merriam-webster.com/dictionary/commit
[78] Psalm 37:5 NLT
[79] Romans 8:32 ESV
[80] Romans 10:13 ESV
[81] 1 Timothy 1:16 NLT
[82] Psalm 37:23 TLB
[83] Psalm 16:11 AMP

It's Yours to Take

[84] Exodus 14, any version. I highly don't recommend any King James version because noneth of thousest talkest in a manner such as written in this modern day. NLT or NIV provide a much more gripping read.
[85] https://en.wikipedia.org/wiki/List_of_sharks_in_the_Red_Sea https://www.scuba-travel.co.uk/redsea/redsealife.html
[86] Hillsong Young & Free, "Highs and Lows"
[87] Dr. Kulreet Chaudhary, *Sound Medicine: How to Use the Ancient Science of Sound to Heal the Body and Mind*
[88] Exodus 14:14 NIV
[89] 1 Peter 5:10 NLT
[90] James 4:8 ESV

PS

[91] Isaiah 7:11 NIV
[92] Romans 10:12b–13 NIV
[93] Romans 10:9 NIV
[94] Exodus 14:21 NIV

ABOUT THE AUTHOR

BEKAH DEIFILIA IS JUST AN average person who works an average job and has average hobbies. But extraordinary things can start in ordinary places. And floating in the sea of mediocrity lies someone with a burning desire to bring light and help others find their way out of their own dark places.

She hopes her story encourages and strengthens you, dear reader.

Ingram Content Group UK Ltd.
Milton Keynes UK
UKHW010657120323
418424UK00001B/135